BACKROADS & BYWAYS
OF
INDIAN
COUNTRY

CONTENTS

ACKNOWLEDGMENTS

This book wouldn't have been possible without the help and support of many people, especially my husband, Jerry, who served as part-time chauffeur and full-time IT support. Without him, 90 percent of the photos that appear in this book would have fallen prey to a computer virus three days before my deadline. I know, Jerry—if I backed things up on the server, or even a CD, it would make your life a whole lot easier.

I also owe a special thanks as well to my daughters, Kelly and Kim, who sacrificed three solid weeks to drive the backroads of Arizona, Colorado, New Mexico, and Utah and who had to fend for themselves while I was on the road or holed up in front of my laptop. Next summer, we'll vacation at a slower pace, I promise.

Others played an important role in the researching, writing, and completion of this book. Thanks to my family and friends, who encouraged me, and to all of the wonderful people I met along the way, including Hopi anthropologist Micah Loma'omvaya, James Surveyor, and the Native Americans who guided me through their sacred lands. I also want to recognize Mike Finney, Alexa Gunther, and Kathie Curley for their help in planning my itineraries, as well as the Albuquerque, Durango, Farmington, and Flagstaff Convention and Visitors Bureaus for their input.

And to the people I haven't seen in what feels like months, we'll get together soon. Lunch is on me.

A tour group hikes past pictographs in the Ute Mountain Tribal Park.
Matt Inden of Weaver Multimedia Group and the Colorado Tourism Office

INTRODUCTION

My first encounter with Native American culture was a bite of hot, donut-like fry bread dusted with powdered sugar. I can't remember where I first ate this treat or even when—maybe one of the few times we made it to the Arizona State Fair—but it became a fixture in my childhood. Winters, when it was cool enough to fry inside, my mother would follow the recipe from an Arizona cookbook and shape the dough into balls that she would fry to golden brown. I remember watching the bread puff, anticipating our meal of what is today referred to as an Indian taco.

Only later, as an adult, did I realize my fry bread had a story. In retaliation for repeated attacks, the United States Army launched a scorched-earth campaign against the Navajo, burning their fields, destroying their orchards, poisoning their wells, and either killing or confiscating their livestock. By December 1863, the starving Navajos had had enough, and, believing Christopher "Kit" Carson's promise that they would be well fed, they surrendered. Carson then marched them at gunpoint almost 300 miles to Fort Sumner.

Nearly 200 people died from cold and starvation on the Long Walk, and when they arrived at their new home, they quickly learned the promised food didn't exist. The water was brackish, the corn crop became infested with worms, and what little outside food did arrive was often spoiled. Forced to feed their families with what little resources they did have, Navajo women used Army-issue white flour, salt, baking powder, and lard to create fry bread. The Navajo and other reservation tribes adopted the meal, making it a Native American staple.

Fry bread taught me that when it comes to the Native Americans of the Southwest, past or present, what seems straightforward can often have a complicated history, layers of meaning, or several interpretations. Places can have multiple names with multiple spellings of the same name. Neighbors can disagree on what should be shared with outsiders and what is taboo. Even the stories behind historical events can vary slightly depending on whether Anglos,

Southern Utah

Hispanics, or Native Americans relay what happened. And that makes touring Indian Country different than visiting Boston or the Grand Canyon.

But what really separates the Indian Country of the Southwest from other destinations is its beauty and the warmth of the people who live here. Some of the most iconic images of the Southwest can be found in this region: Monument Valley, Antelope Canyon, Bryce Canyon, and Mesa Verde. People you have met only minutes before in a village will invite you into their homes. In all the travels I completed for this book, the highlight for me was an invite from an 80-year-old Hopi medicine man to share his cupcakes and Kool-Aid.

I set out to make the Native American lands and people of the Four Corners region accessible to the average traveler. As you drive the backroads and byways of Indian Country, you'll leave behind the traffic and troubles of everyday American life. You'll walk through rooms inhabited by Ancestral Puebloan Indians 900 years ago, stand over the edge of the Grand Canyon, and ride a narrow gauge railroad through traditional hunting grounds. You'll also enter villages that have been inhabited for centuries and, if you're lucky, witness ceremonial dances on the plaza.

Since some of these areas are remote, I've provided suggestions at the end of each chapter for linking one drive to another or exploring an area further. Additionally, the appendix lists ruins, petroglyph sites, museums, cultural center, and trading posts throughout the Southwest that weren't included on the drives in this book. If you have the time, I encourage you to explore these as well. One thing I learned while writing this book is that the Indian Country destinations that first come to mind, like Chaco Canyon or Mesa Verde, are only the tip of the iceberg. There is so much more to explore in this often-overlooked region.

Before you head out, though, read "Things to Know." This section details the etiquette to follow when visiting ruins and villages, and it provides information on issues like weather, driving conditions, and time zones. The section also provides helpful information on how to select a tour guide, tipping, and purchasing arts and crafts.

The backroads and byways of Indian Country offer beautiful landscapes, a rich history, and the hospitality of a people whose ancestors have inhabited the region for hundreds and, in some cases, thousands of years. As you travel, be open to new experiences. Listen to the stories and make an effort to learn more about the tribes you visit. You'll be rewarded with an unforgettable experience.

Teresa Bitler
Phoenix, Arizona

Cliff dwellings in Mesa Verde National Park

THINGS TO KNOW

NAMES OF PLACES

As you prepare for a drive through Indian Country, you'll become familiar with the names of places you want to visit. Don't be surprised when you study a map or reference another resource if the name is slightly different. For example, Old Oraibi might be referred to as *Orayvi*. Or, the Hopi village of Moenkopi might be *Munqapi*. In many cases, the differences can be attributed to an Americanization of a Native American word.

You'll also find that some places have more than one name: a common name and one or more Native American names. Window Rock is *Tségháhoodzání,* which means Perforated Rock. Nearby St. Michael is known as *Ts'íhootso* or Yellow Meadow while Crownpoint, New Mexico, goes by two names: *T'ííst'óóz Ndeesh-gizh* or Narrow-Leafed Cottonwood Gap, and *T'iists'ózí* or Slender Cottonwood.

Chances are you'll never hear the native name for a place or even see it on a map, but it's good to keep in mind that some places have more than one name and some can be spelled in various ways.

WEATHER

Temperatures vary depending on elevation, but most of the area covered in this book is located on the Colorado Plateau, which is classified as arid. Although its desert areas receive on average less than 10 inches of rain each year, that does-n't mean it doesn't rain here or that you'll never encounter severe weather. From July through August, the region experiences thunderstorms, known locally as monsoons, which can cause flashfloods. If you're in wash or canyon, you and your car could be swept away. Pay attention to the weather, and if a wash has water in it already, do not cross. It may be deeper than you think.

In the winter, higher elevations in the Four Corners area get snow. Check the weather before you leave, and dress appropriately. You may also want to check road conditions for road closures and to see if chains are required.

During the summer, you'll have to deal with the other extreme. In desert areas, the temperature can soar over 100 degrees. There may be little or no shade. Wear sunscreen and bring plenty of water. Remember: some of these sites are very remote, and even though they may be designated a national park or monument, that doesn't mean they have food, water, or gas.

Also, since many of the destinations in this book are located at higher elevations, take precautions to avoid altitude sickness. For your first day in the area, schedule less strenuous activities like visiting museums instead of skiing or hiking. You'll also want to drink plenty of water and avoid too much alcohol. The good news is that eating carbohydrates helps prevent the ill effects of high altitude, so go ahead and order the pasta and breadsticks. You're on vacation, after all.

ROAD CONDITIONS

This book tackles the backroads and byways of Indian Country. For the most part, you'll drive on paved roads, but at times, you'll be directed off the beaten path. Chaco Canyon is a good example. So is Grand Canyon West. Most vehicles should be able to handle the washboard roads without a problem.

But you should understand that not all Country Roads and Indian Routes are maintained. Don't randomly pick a road and strike out exploring, for several reasons. First, some of the roads require four-wheel drive. Second, on reservations, if you head out without a guide and end up somewhere you're not supposed to be, you will be escorted out of the area and possibly off the reservation. Third, there are no services once you're off the highway. You can't drive to Chaco Canyon and expect to be able to fill your gas tank. There isn't a gas station. And, if you run out of gas, you may not have cell service.

As you drive through Indian Country, animals are another hazard you might encounter. On reservations, it's not uncommon for free-roaming animals to wander into the road. I've seen sheep, goats, cows, horses, and shepherds' dogs in the road during my travels. And domesticated animals aren't the only problem. Wildlife often darts across the road in remote areas. Keep alert for deer, elk, and coyotes, at the very least.

VISITING RUINS

Common sense should prevail when visiting ruins. Don't touch anything, since the oils from your skin can damage the stones, plaster, petroglyphs (images carved into the sandstone), and pictographs (images painted on the canyon walls). Technically, if you see something on the ground, like a pottery shard, you can pick

Exploring an ancient kiva in Mesa Verde National Park *Matt Inden of Weaver Multimedia Group and the Colorado Tourism Office*

it up as long as you return it to exactly the same place. Still, it's best not to, because again, the oils on your hands can damage whatever you find.

You also shouldn't use the area as a recreational site. Don't camp in or around the ruins. Campfire smoke stains walls and the surrounding rocks and cliffs. Also, avoid eating anything at the site. Crumbs attract rodents that can cause damage. You shouldn't hike or wander off marked trails either, since you could be stepping on ruins buried under the dirt and not even know it.

Finally, don't leave offerings. You may think you're honoring the culture of an ancient people, but your actions could be interpreted as offensive.

VILLAGE ETIQUETTE

When you enter a village, above all else be respectful. Keep in mind that you've entered the residents' home, and they have rules they ask that you follow. First, do not bring alcohol, drugs, or firearms onto the reservation or into their village. Sometimes, pets are not welcome either.

Also, let them know you're visiting by checking in at the visitor center, which is usually clearly marked and easy to find. Why? The village might be closed while the tribe prepares for a ceremony or special event. Your stop at the center is also an opportunity for the tribe to explain what's off limits or unacceptable while visiting, as well as a chance for you to purchase a camera permit, if one is available.

While talking at the visitor center, you may learn about ceremonies or dances in the village that day. If you are invited to attend, put your camera away. Even if you purchased a camera permit, you will not be permitted to photograph, videotape, or record the ceremony in any way. Position yourself near the back of the onlookers or, if you are invited, on a rooftop. The chairs lining the plaza are reserved for tribe members. And, obviously, don't talk loudly or cause a distraction during the performance.

PHOTOGRAPHS

Generally, you *are* allowed to photograph ruins; you *are not* allowed to photograph ceremonies, villages, or Native Americans, except under certain circumstances. If you are attending a traditional ceremony, you won't be allowed to take photographs or record the event electronically in any way, as mentioned above; in addition, you won't be permitted to take notes or make sketches. However, in some instances, professional dancers performing in a public setting, such as at a cultural center, may permit photographs.

Some villages prohibit any recording of their way of life. Don't test this. Tribal authorities or elders can seize your camera, and you may not get it back. Other villages allow you to purchase a camera permit, which will usually cost $5–10. Sometimes, it's worth it (I took a lot of photos at Acoma Pueblo); other times it's not (there really wasn't anything to photograph at Zuni Pueblo). Before you buy the permit, get a feel for the village and what you might like to photograph. Then, discuss restrictions with the cashier at the visitor center to determine whether the permit is worth it.

Even if you have a permit, there will be limits to what you can photograph. Again, forget the dances or ceremonies. You also won't be able to photograph any tribe member without asking their permission first. The same with their crafts. Ask before you take a picture. While most of the time, it's okay to capture images of buildings, you may be asked not to photograph homes or animals either.

GUIDES

To visit some destinations, like Antelope Canyon, you need to hire a Native American guide. In other places, like Monument Valley Navajo Tribal Park, you may not *need* a guide, but by hiring one, you'll see more. Either way, if you want a guide, it's best to make arrangements before you go.

Keep in mind that some guides work on a cash-only basis, and you will be expected to tip your guide. Tips should be in line with what you'd tip at a restaurant, 15–20 percent, but there is no set rule.

At the end of each chapter that includes sites where you'll need or want a guide, I've included a section listing available companies.

The cliff dwellings in Mesa Verde National Park
Matt Inden of Weaver Multimedia Group and the Colorado Tourism Office

1 Canyons of the Ancients

Estimated length: 90 miles, roundtrip to Cortez

Estimated time: 3 hours, roundtrip to Cortez

Getting there: From I-40, near Gallup, take Exit 20, and head north on US 491 for approximately 95 miles to Shiprock. Then, continue into Cortez. From I-70, west of Grand Junction, turn south on US 191, driving past Arches National Park and through Moab. After 1.5 hours, you'll enter Monticello. Turn left at US 491 and follow it for 60 miles into Cortez.

Highlights: Mile for mile, if you want to see Ancestral Puebloan ruins, you can't beat the drive through Canyons of the Ancients National Monument. Along the way, you will visit Hovenweep National Monument, Lowery Pueblo, Painted Hand Pueblo, and Mesa Verde National Park. You can learn about these ancient dwellers at the Crow Canyon Archaeological Center and the Anasazi Heritage Center. The route also offers a respite for the weary at the tasting rooms of McElmo Canyon's wineries.

Even though you will spend just 2.5 hours on the road, set aside a full day to take in all the sites along the way. Strike out from Cortez south on US 491 and turn right on County Road G. On the left, you'll pass the Cortez Municipal Airport.

Approximately 3.5 miles down the road, on the right side, you'll see a small white sign for Guy Drew Vineyards. If you started out first thing in the morning, you may have to come back later—winemaker Guy Drew pours tastes at the vineyard daily 12–5. Sample the Metate, a red blend named after the grinding stones

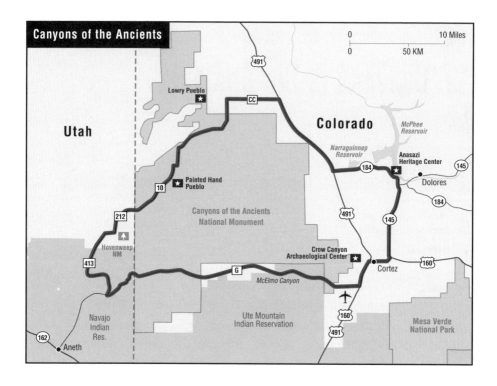

found on the property, then pick up a bottle to bring home and move on to **Sutcliffe Vineyards**. Located 10 miles down the road, the picturesque property produces wines that consistently garner praise from *Wine Spectator*.

Just before Sutcliffe Vineyards, you pass the Sand Canyon Trailhead, part of

The Sand Canyon Trailhead at Canyon of the Ancients National Monument

the **Canyons of the Ancients National Monument**. The one-way hike begins at the sliprock surface parking lot, north of County Road G in McElmo Canyon, and ends 6.5 miles later at Sand Canyon Pueblo, one of the largest Ancient Puebloan settlements in the area with 420 rooms, 100 kivas, and 14 towers. (Don't expect to see massive ruins on a par with those of Chaco Canyon or Mesa Verde, though, since the pueblo today has no

Take a break from touring ruins at Guy Drew Vineyards.

exposed walls.) If you want to hike the entire trail, you are encouraged to park one car at the McElmo Canyon trailhead and to park another at Sand Canyon Pueblo. Or you can limit yourself to Castle Rock Pueblo, located just beyond the parking area, and the several small cliff dwellings a short way up the canyon.

County Road G becomes County Road 402/Ismay Trading Post Road when you cross from Colorado into Utah. The Utah road takes its name from a small trading post near the state border. Less than 4 miles into Utah, a road sign directs you toward **Hovenweep National Monument**. Turn right off County Road 402 onto County Road 401. Follow this another 4 miles to County Road 413. Warning: the roads in this area have multiple names, some changing from one road number to another for no apparent reason. Don't worry. The route is well marked, and it is easy to find your way to Hovenweep.

As you drive to the visitor center, note the arid lands of the Great Sage Plain. Nomadic hunter gatherers first visited the area 10,000 years ago, but it wasn't until 900 A.D. that people began to settle here, building the Hovenweep structures between 1200 and 1300 A.D. The trails from the visitor center lead you along the rim of Little Ruin Canyon and past the Square Tower Group ruins. It's a 1.5-hour

TRAIL OF THE ANCIENTS, OR CANYON OF THE ANCIENTS?

On this drive, you'll be in Canyon of the Ancients and on Trail of the Ancients. Where does one begin and the other end?

Trail of the Ancients is the only National Scenic Byway dedicated solely to archaeology. It includes Navajo National Monument, Monument Valley, Valley of the Gods, Edge of the Cedars State Park, Hovenweep National Monument, Canyon de Chelly National Monument, and Mesa Verde National Park. The byway isn't a specific route that takes you from Point A to Point B. Instead, it covers the entire Four Corners region.

Canyon of the Ancients is a national monument encompassing approximately 183,000 acres of land. It contains the highest known density of archaeological sites in the nation—up to 100 per square mile in some places. Archaeologists actually estimate that, although there are only 6,000 recorded sites so far, there may be as many as 30,000 sites total. Canyon of the Ancients includes portions of Hovenweep National Monument, Painted Hand Pueblo, Lowry Pueblo, and Sand Canyon Pueblo.

hike, with a steep trail in and out. Highlights include Hovenweep Castle, Hovenweep House, and the Twin Towers.

The Square Tower Group is one of six villages protected by the National Park Service at Hovenweep National Monument. In addition to these, the nearby Canyon of the Ancients National Monument boasts 6,355 recorded archaeological sites as well as up to 20,000 undiscovered sites. If you want to access some of these remote locations, talk to the ranger at the visitor center or inquire at the Anasazi Heritage Center later on the drive. While many of these ruins are open to the public, their precise locations are not publicized, and the roads leading to them are un-

Several of Hovenweep's most famous structures are located in Little Ruins Canyon.

paved and rough. Take plenty of water and make sure you have a full tank of gas before you go. Four-wheel drive wouldn't hurt either.

From Hovenweep, turn right. The next 20 miles take about 40 minutes to drive because even though the road is paved, cattle guards and the occasional curve force you to slow down. Spend the time taking in the scenery. The rock and sage near the national monument eventually gives way to irrigated farmland, so even though you haven't gone very far in that time, it will feel like you have. And, watch for the unmarked dirt road on the right that leads to **Painted Hand Pueblo**, the Ancestral Puebloan ruins of a small village.

Sixteen miles after leaving Hovenweep, you have a decision to make. You can continue straight toward **Lowry Pueblo** or turn at County Road BB. If you opt for the latter, it's 4 miles to US 491. However, if you have the time, drive 1 mile north to County Road CC and turn left. The Lowry ruins are 3 miles on the left, easy to locate, and feature two kivas. Archaeologists speculate that the Lowry Great Kiva

---

WHAT NOT TO DO AT AN ARCHAEOLOGICAL SITE
or, ANCESTRAL PUEBLOAN ETIQUETTE

Canyon of the Ancients National Monument is a collection of more than 6,000 documented archaeological sites and tens of thousands undocumented sites. Mesa Verde National Park contains more than 4,700 documented sites. To preserve these sites and any others you visit during your travels, follow these simple rules:

❖ *Don't touch anything.* Skin oil damages ruins, petroglyphs, pictographs, and plaster.

❖ *Don't dig.* You're not an archaeologist. Leave artifacts in their original context.

❖ *Don't wander off.* Stay on clearly marked trails and roads.

❖ *Don't picnic.* Save the snacks for the car. Crumbs attract rodents that can cause damage.

❖ *Don't camp.* Campfire smoke stains walls and cliffs.

❖ *Don't leave offerings.* Respect the spiritual significance these sites hold for Native Americans.

Square Tower in Hovenweep National Monument

was probably a ceremonial gathering place for Ancestral Puebloans within several hundred square miles.

You can take County Road CC back to US 491. Exit Lowry Pueblo to the right and continue until the county road intersects the highway at Pleasant View. Take another right and continue to CO 184, where you'll turn toward the town of Dolores. On your left, you'll pass Narraguinnep Reservoir and McPhee Reservoir, a popular destination for camping, boating, and fishing.

Before you reach Dolores, you'll see the Anasazi Heritage Center on your left. Don't miss this one; it's a must before heading to the Mesa Verde ruins. The museum explores the culture and history of the Ancestral Puebloans, who were called the Anasazi, or ancient ones, by the Navajo

THE LAW

The Archaeological Resources Protection Act of 1979 and the Antiquities Act of 1906 prohibit anyone from removing or disturbing archaeological sites or artifacts on federal public lands without written permission from the Department of the Interior.

that later settled in the region. Weave on a Puebloan loom, grind corn meal on a metate, examine specimens through microscopes and handle actual artifacts. A life-size replica demonstrates what the pithouses at Mesa Verde would have looked like more than 1,000 years ago when they were occupied.

The Anasazi Heritage Center maintains two archaeological sites on its grounds. Escalante Pueblo, a rectangular block of 28 rooms surrounding a kiva, is located at the end of a half-mile, wheelchair-accessible trail near the museum, while the four-room Dominguez site sits at the base of the hill below. The two sites were named for the Spanish explorers, Escalante and Dominguez, that made note of them in 1776.

You can continue on CO 184 toward Cortez. Be careful, though, to stay to the right when it hooks up with CO 145—head south toward Cortez on CO 145, not east towards Dolores.

In Cortez, tour the Cortez Cultural Center and Hawkins Preserve. Housed in a historic 1909 building in downtown Cortez, the cultural center offers Native American exhibits, an authentic hogan, a replica Ancestral Puebloan ruin and an art gallery featuring local artists. It also hosts a variety of seasonal programs, in-

The ruins of Hovenweep National Monument

ANASAZI OR ANCESTRAL PUEBLOAN?

If you haven't visited a Native American museum or the ruins of ancient Indian cultures lately, you may be surprised to hear the term *Ancestral Puebloan* instead of *Anasazi*. Recently, the National Park Service, anthropologists, and others have begun using *Ancestral Puebloan* to describe the people that lived on the Colorado Plateau between the year 1 and 1300 A.D. Why? The Navajo word *'Ana'i* was thought to mean "old ones" when it was originally coined but is now understood to mean "enemy ancestors." *Ancestral Puebloan* is understood to be more respectful, if not entirely accurate.

---

cluding Native American dances, artist demonstrations, storytellers, music programs, and lectures. Check online for a current schedule. The staff at the cultural center can also provide information on the area's Ancestral Puebloan ruin sites

and direct you to the Hawkins Preserve, a 122-acre tract of land on the south side of Cortez where you can hike, rock climb with a permit, and view wildlife here. Hawkins Preserve also has three documented Ancestral Puebloan sites.

The **Crow Canyon Archaeological Center** is for anyone who has ever dreamed of excavating Ancestral Puebloan ruins. On the day tour, you examine artifacts, tour the laboratory, eat lunch and then visit the current excavation site. Weeklong programs allow you to work alongside the center's archaeologists, digging at the site or analyzing artifacts in the laboratory. The center has family programs, summer camps, and field programs for high school and middle school students.

A replica pithouse at the Anasazi Heritage Center

The Anasazi Heritage Center gives a good overview of the local ancestral tribes.
Matt Inden of Weaver Multimedia Group and the Colorado Tourism Office

While you are in Cortez, make a point to visit the **Notah Dineh Trading Company**. In addition to an extensive collection of rugs and other Native American arts and crafts, the trading post houses a museum where you can see antique cradleboards, moccasins, tomahawks, breastplates, pottery, kachina dolls from the 1920s, and other artifacts. Western relics like antique bridles and historic firearms are also on display as is the largest known Two Grey Hills rug, a 12-foot by 18-foot design.

Set aside at least a day to explore **Mesa Verde National Park**. From downtown Cortez, head east on US 160 to CO 10, the entrance to the park. After 9 miles of winding road and hairpin turns, you'll arrive at the Far View Visitor Center where you can purchase tickets for the ranger-led tours to Cliff Palace, Balcony House, and Long House. Tickets do sell out, so get there early and be prepared to stand in line. A gift shop and exhibits on the Ancestral Puebloans should keep other members of your party occupied while you make tour arrangements.

Tickets in hand, plan your day around your scheduled tour. If you have some time before you need to check in with the guide, start at the ancient farming community of **Far View**, the first ruin site on Chapin Mesa. Mummy Lake, the artificial reservoir that stored water for Far View farmers, is considered by some to be one of the more unique structures in Mesa Verde. The site also includes three houses, Coyote Village, and Far View Tower.

Before you get to Cliff Palace, stop first at **Chapin Mesa Museum** and **Spruce Tree House**. The museum shows a 25-minute orientation film and displays dioramas of Ancestral Puebloan life. Although it houses an impressive collection of prehistoric artifacts and crafts, it feels dated. If you've visit the Anasazi Heritage Center and need to be selective on your Mesa Verde trip, you can cut your tour of the museum short or skip it altogether. But, do hike the short trail behind the museum to Spruce Tree House, the best preserved cliff dwelling in the park. The

An archeologist works near the town of Cortez *Matt Inden of Weaver Multimedia Group and the Colorado Tourism Office*

Tourists on a ranger-led tour of Cliff Palace

self-guided and ranger-led tours to the ruins are free, and you can climb down into an actual kiva.

You'll probably recognize **Cliff Palace** as you peer down at the largest cliff dwelling in the park—it's an iconic Southwestern image. Expect the parking lot to be crowded since it's also the most popular tour. One right after the other, rangers guide visitors down a series of steps to the ruins where they explain the history and culture of the Ancient Puebloans. Unlike your visit to the Spruce Tree House, this tour limits how much time you can spend at the ruins. It is well worth the trip, but you will move from Point A to Point B as a group.

The road loops around from Cliff Palace to **Balcony House**, which also requires a ticket to tour, and returns you just south of Chapin Mesa Museum. Turn left and continue to the **Mesa Top Loop**. Although the Mesa Loop ruins lack the grandeur of Cliff Palace, they demonstrate the evolution of Ancestral Puebloan structures, beginning with pithouses and progressing to the Sun Temple. If you made it to the Anasazi Heritage Center before coming to Mesa Verde, you can vi-

You can take a self-guided tour at Spruce Tree House.

sualize what life in these pithouses must have been like for the Puebloans.

Make your way back to the Far View Visitor Center. Just before you get to the parking lot, you'll see a turnoff for Wetherill Mesa Road. Open from late May until early September, this road takes you to **Step House** and **Long House**. Vehicles are restricted to less than 8,000 pounds (gross vehicle weight) and less than 25 feet in length. Also, note that near the ruins, you will need to park and board a tram to get to the actual sites. However, the ruins at Wetherill Mesa are just as impressive and less crowded.

From Mesa Verde and Cortez, you can easily access several of the other drives. Shiprock, the starting point for the Four Corners drive, is only 40 miles south. Farmington, the end point for the New Mexico Badlands drive, is only 70 miles southeast. And, Durango and the nearby Southern Ute Tribe are only 45 miles away.

Cliff Palace is the largest ruin in Mesa Verde National Park.

IN THE AREA

ACCOMMODATIONS

Best Western Turquoise Inn & Suites, 535 E. Main Street, Cortez. Call 970-565-3778 or 1-800-547-3376. Located conveniently in the heart of Cortez, this pet-friendly hotel offers a free continental breakfast. Rates begin at $84.95 in the winter and range up to $175 during the summer. Web site: www.bestwesternmesaverde.com.

Canyon of the Ancients Guest Ranch, 7986 County Road G, Cortez. Call 970-565-4288. The four Southwestern-themed houses at this ranch include kitchens and wireless Internet and can accommodate four to seven guests. You can rent the houses on a nightly basis (two night minimum), starting at $150 per night, or by the week. Web site: www.canyonofthe ancients.com.

Dunton Hot Springs, Dolores. Call 970-882-4800. Situated in a restored ghost town, this exclusive resort features hand-hewn log cabins, natural hot springs, spa services, and high-speed wireless Internet access. Since it's owned by John Sutcliffe, the man behind Sutcliffe Vineyards, you can guess what they pour at dinner. Winter rates begin at $500/night, summer rates at $850/night. Meals are included. Web site: www.dutonhot springs.com.

Far View Lodge, 1 Navajo Hill, Mesa Verde Park. Call 1-866-875-8456. As the only lodging available within the park, Far View Lodge delivers basic accommodations beginning at $100 per night. Don't miss the onsite restaurant, The Metate Room, which is renowned for its Native American-inspired cuisine. Web site: www.visit mesaverde.com.

Holiday Inn Express Mesa Verde–Cortez, 2121 E. Main Street, Cortez. Call 877-859-5095. This highly rated Holiday Inn Express offers a complimentary breakfast, indoor pool, and fitness center. Web site: www.colorado holiday.com.

Kelly Place Bed & Breakfast, 14537 County Road G, Cortez. Call 970-565-3125 or 1-800-745-4885. Built by horticulturists George and Sue Kelly in the 1960s as their retirement home, this property offers seven lodge rooms and three adobe-style cabins. Rates start at $72 per night, with a $20 premium April through October, and include a full country-style breakfast. During your stay, take the self-guided tour of the property's prehistoric Indian sites and ruins. Web site: www.kellyplace.com.

Tomahawk Lodge, 728 S. Broadway, Cortez. Call 970-565-8521. This 50s-era motel is a clean and comfortable bargain at $45–95/night. Web site: www.angelfire.com/co2/tomahawk.

ATTRACTIONS AND RECREATION

Anasazi Heritage Center, 27501 CO 184, Dolores. Call 970-882-5600. This is one of the area's best museums, especially for kids, who can weave on a Pueblo-style loom, grind corn, and touch real artifacts. There's also a replica pithouse. Outside, visit the Escalante Pueblo and Dominguez Pueblo ruins. The center is open March through October, daily 9–5; November through February, daily 10–4. Admission is $3/adults, free for children 17 and under. Web site: www.co.blm.gov/ahc.

Canyons of the Ancients National Monument, headquartered in the Anasazi Heritage Center, 27501 CO 184, Dolores. Web site: www.co.blm .gov/canm.

Cortez Cultural Center and Hawkins Preserve, 25 N. Market Street, Cortez. Call 970-565-1151. The cultural center has an indoor museum, replica ancestral Pueblo ruin, and authentic hogan, and it hosts a variety of seasonal programs, including art exhibits, lectures, festivals and Native American dancers. It also maintains the 122-acre Hawkins Preserve, an ideal spot for hiking and birding. The Hawkins Preserve has three Ancestral Puebloan ruins as well. Web site: www.cortezculturalcenter.org.

Crow Canyon Archaeological Center, 23390 Road K, Cortez. Call 970-565-8975 or 1-800-422-8975. Visitors can

The Mesa Top Loop takes you past pithouses and pueblos.

work alongside professional archaeologists during weeklong summer programs or take a day tour of the center, including a visit to the laboratory and current excavation site. Web site: www.crowcanyon.org.

Guy Drew Vineyards, 20057 County Road G, Cortez. Call 970-565-4958. Complimentary tastings daily 12–5. Web site: www.guydrewvineyards .com.

Hovenweep National Monument, located along the McElmo Route/County Road 401. Call 970-562-4282, ext. 10. An easy, 1.5-mile hike takes you past well-preserved ancestral Pueblo ruins, including Hovenweep Castle and several towers. The site is open daily 8–5. Admission is $3/person or $6/vehicle. Web site: www.nps .gov/hove.

Lowry Pueblo, located on County Road CC, off SR 491. This site has approximately 40 rooms and eight kivas, including a great kiva that is nearly 50 feet in diameter.

McPhee Reservoir, CO 184. Just 10 miles north of Cortez and 8 miles west of Dolores, this recreation area has a campground and boat ramp and is stocked with rainbow trout.

Mesa Verde National Park, CO 160. Call 970-529-4465. Approximately 4,700 known archeological sites, including 600 cliff dwellings, dot the landscape of this renowned national park. Expect to pay $15/car during summer months, $10/car during winter to enter and additional for guided tours, like the one to Mesa Verde's largest cliff dwelling, Cliff Palace. Hours are seasonal, and tour rates vary. Web site: www.nps.gov/meve. Highlights at the park include:

❖ **Balcony House:** Rangers lead tours to this smaller dwelling, which requires you to climb multiple ladders and crawl through a 12-foot long tunnel.

❖ **Chapin Mesa Museum:** View dioramas depicting Ancestral Puebloans life, watch an orientation film and observe Native American artifacts.

❖ **Cliff Palace:** The largest and well-known of the ruins. You can view from above or take a ranger-led tour.

❖ **Far View:** This farming community has five sites and a reservoir.

❖ **Long House:** Located on the Wetherill Mesa, the second largest cliff dwelling in the park can be observed from an overlook or up close on a ranger-led tour (summer only).

❖ **Mesa Top Loop:** Take in 600 years of Puebloan development on an easy drive with short, paved walkways to the sites.

❖ **Step House:** A self-guided trail takes you to an alcove with several pithouses and a cliff dwelling.

❖ **Spruce Tree House:** The best preserved of the cliff dwellings, this site allows visitors to climb into an actual kiva.

Notah Dineh Trading Company and Museum, 345 West Main, Cortez. Call 1-800-444-2024. The trading post features the largest collection of Navajo rugs in the Four Corners region, including designs such as Two Grey Hills and Ganado Red. In the museum, you'll see antique cradleboards, moccasins, tomahawks, breastplates, pottery, kachinas from the 1920s, and Western relics. It also displays the largest known Two Grey Hills rug, a 12-foot by 18-foot design. Free.

Painted Hand Pueblo, on Bureau of Land Management Road 4531. Visit the Canyons of the Ancients National Monument for specific directions and details.

Sutcliffe Vineyards, 12202 County Road G, Cortez. Call 970-565-0825. These world-class wines come from grapes grown on the property—not shipped in from elsewhere. Web site: www.sutcliffewines.com.

DINING

Dry Dock Restaurant & Pub, 200 W. Main Street, Cortez. Call 970-564-9404. A local favorite, this restaurant serves aged beef and fresh seafood. Open for dinner. Web site: www.the drydock.com.

Francisca's Restaurant, 125 E. Main Street, Cortez. Call 970-565-4093. The restaurant specializes in Mexican fare like fajitas and chile rellenos.

J. Fargo's Family Dining & Micro Brewery, 1209 E. Main Street, Cortez. Call 970-564-0242. The extensive menu at this casual, family-friendly establishment includes burgers, pizza, steaks, salads, and Southwestern favorites. Plus, there's microbrewed beer on tap. Open daily for breakfast, lunch, and dinner. Web site: www.jfargos.com.

Metate Room Restaurant, 1 Navajo Hill, Mesa Verde Park. Located at the Far View Lodge in Mesa Verde National Park, The Metate Room adds Native American flavor to a contemporary menu. Open for dinner.

Nero's Restaurant, 303 W. Main Street, Cortez. Call 970-565-7366. Chef Richard Gurd, a graduate of the Culinary Institute of American, serves upscale fare and Italian dishes. Open daily for lunch and dinner.

Silver Bean, 410 W. Main Street, Cortez. Call 970-946-4404. You can't miss the vintage silver Airstream surrounded by a white picket fence, artificial grass, and pink flamingos. The coffee is great, of course, but so are the breakfast burritos. Open Monday through Saturday.

OTHER CONTACTS

Colorado Welcome Center, 928 E. Main Street, Cortez. Call 970-565-4048.

Mesa Verde Country Visitor Information Bureau, Cortez. Call 970-565-8227. The bureau's online resources include maps, itineraries, a calendar and information on local attractions, lodging, dining, shopping, and more. Web site: www.mesaverdecountry .com.

Mesa Verde Colorado. Call 800-449-2288. Aramark Parks and Destinations provides the national park's management services like dining and lodging. Visit their Web site for listings on where to stay, where to eat and what tour to take. Web site: www.visitmesaverde.com.

San Juan County. Call 1-800-574-4386. The county's Web site provides helpful information on planning a trip in the area. Web site: www.utahscanyoncountry.com.

Trail of the Ancients. The route runs through Canyon of the Ancients and highlights many of the same destinations on this drive. Web site: www.trailoftheancients.com

Shiprock Pinnacle *New Mexico Tourism Department and Mike Stauffer*

2 Standing in Four States at Once

Estimated length: 75 miles, roundtrip to Shiprock

Estimated time: 1.5 hours, roundtrip to Shiprock

Getting there: From I-40, near Gallup, take Exit 20, and head north on US 491 for approximately 95 miles to Shiprock. From Albuquerque, take I-25 North to US 550 and head west toward Farmington. At Bloomfield, turn left onto US 64. Drive through Farmington and continue for approximately 30 miles.

Highlights: Pose for photographs while standing in four states at once on this loop that starts and ends in Shiprock, New Mexico. Along the way, you'll glimpse Shiprock Pinnacle, visit historic trading posts and tour the Ancestral Puebloan ruins of the Ute Mountain Ute Reservation. Extend your visit in the area by driving north to Cortez to explore Canyon of the Ancients National Monument and Mesa Verde National Park.

One word best describes Shiprock and the drive that loops past the Four Corners Monument: remote. Cell phone reception is limited, and you will need to start out from Shiprock with a full tank of gas and water because services along the way are nearly nonexistent. However, this region where Arizona, Colorado, New Mexico, and Utah meet provides an opportunity to experience rural Navajoland and, if you decide to take a short detour north, the Ute Mountain Ute tribe.

The drive begins in Shiprock, the largest community in the Navajo Nation. Founded in 1903 when the U.S. government established the San Juan School and Agency here, the community was originally called *Naat'áanii Nééz,* or Tall Boss, by the Navajo, in honor of William T. Shelton, the superintendent of the Bureau

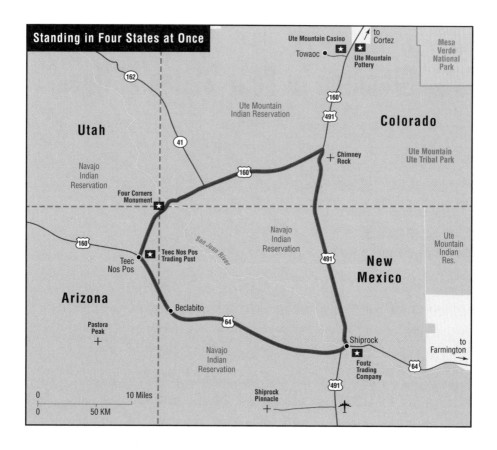

of Indian Affairs. Over the years, Shelton opened a boarding school in town, improved the existing irrigation system, initiated the Shiprock Fair (now called the Northern Navajo Nation Fair), and opened a coalmine nearby. The agency later took the name of the rock formation 9 miles southwest and became known as the Shiprock Agency.

As you explore the town, you'll find there isn't much for tourists. Shiprock consists of the Northern Navajo Medical Center, a Diné College campus, the fairgrounds, retail outlets, gas stations, and fast food. The Foutz Trading Company, however, is the exception. Located on US 64, a mile east of the San Juan River Bridge, the trading post stocks rugs, pottery, kachinas, sand paintings, sculptures, drums, and Native American folk art.

From Foutz Trading Company, head west on US 64. Cross the San Juan River Bridge and continue for about half a mile to where US 491 and US 64 split. It's an easy intersection to miss, so watch for the Shiprock Quick Mart, which will be on the northwest corner of the intersection. Across the street, on the right, you'll see a Shell; up ahead, on the left, is a McDonalds. Turn right at this intersection. You'll know you're headed in the correct direction if you pass Shiprock High School on the left a half mile down the road.

The next 25 miles unfold as a classic Western landscape with a usually blue sky meeting the open desert plain at the horizon. To the left, you can clearly see Shiprock Pinnacle, the remains of a solidified lava core. The Diné (Navajo people) call the pinnacle *Tsé Bit' A'í* or "rock with wings," and they have several stories surrounding it. In one account, the formation is a ship that brought their ancestors to the area; in another, it's a bird that brought them here on its back. Still another story tells of how a medicine man asked the gods to deliver the people from their enemies, and the ground rose, lifting them to safety and creating Shiprock Pinnacle.

It is also believed that the Diné lived on the pinnacle for some time, coming

IS IT REALLY THE FOUR CORNERS?

According to some, Four Corners Monument doesn't indicate the precise location where Arizona, Colorado, New Mexico and Utah meet. In fact, it could be up to 2.5 miles off. The U.S. National Geodetic Survey admitted in 2009 that the intersection of the four states is 1,807 feet east of where modern surveyors would mark it, but they also defended the monument's current position.

Part of the debate boils down to an understanding of surveying techniques used in the 1870s. At the time, surveyors used the Washington meridian, the meridian that passes through the Old Naval Observatory, as their reference point instead of the Prime Meridian used today. Based on this, they placed the disputed border between Arizona and New Mexico on the 32nd meridian west of Washington D.C. Global positioning system (GPS) readings, however, indicate that the true location should be northeast of the San Juan River.

So, is the monument in the wrong place? Not according to the United States Supreme Court, which ruled in New Mexico v. Colorado, 267 U.S. 30 (1925), that the monument is exactly where it should be.

THE NORTHERN NAVAJO NATION FAIR

Held in Shiprock every fall, the Northern Navajo Nation Fair is the oldest—it celebrated 100 years in 2011—and most traditional of the Navajo nation's fairs. It began as a way for community members to celebrate the harvest but has grown to include the Miss Northern Navajo Pageant, a rodeo, Indian market, chili cook-off, arts and crafts exhibits, baby pageant, and intertribal powwow. There's also a parade and carnival.

The festivities coincide with *Ye'ii Bi Chei* or "the Night Way," an ancient Navajo healing ceremony that usually takes place after the first frost. You can view parts of this nine-day chant as long as you are respectful, but absolutely no photographs or videos will be permitted.

---

down only to get water and tend to their fields. One day, lightning struck, destroying the trail and leaving only a sheer cliff. The women, children, and elderly stranded on top of the pinnacle had no way down and starved. Because of this, the Diné consider Shiprock Pinnacle very sacred and do not permit hiking or climbing on the pinnacle for fear visitors will disturb the ghosts of their ancestors.

You can get a closer look, though. Instead of turning right to follow US 64, head south 6 miles out of town on US 491. Near the Shiprock Airport, turn left at Indian Route 34. The 7-mile drive takes you to the pinnacle's base. Watch for the lava fence along the way. The 40-foot high phenomenon is actually the remains of lava that flowed into a fissure.

As you continue toward Teec Nos Pos on US 64, you see the Carrizo Mountains and its highest point, Pastora Peak, ahead. For years, prospectors searched this Arizona mountain range for silver and other minerals, finding angry Navajo warriors instead of fortune. Rumors of silver persisted, though. At the turn of the 20th century, George F. Hull leased 640 acres, hired six Navajos at five dollars a day, and conducted a thorough search, according to *Navajo Places: History, Legend, Landscape* by Laurance D. Linford. Hull came up empty-handed. It wasn't until the 1940s that vanadium—an additive that increases the strength of steel—was discovered and mined.

Four miles after you cross the border into Arizona, you enter Teec Nos Pos or *T'iis Názbas,* meaning "cottonwoods in a circle." Roughly 300 people call Teec Nos

Pos home, but you'd estimate only a tenth of that based on what you see: a few houses and the Teec Nos Pos Trading Post. Plan on stopping at the trading post, even if you don't need gas, a soda or another souvenir.

Because the post lacks the glitz of its touristy counterparts, it feels more authentic. Instead of shot glasses and sweatshirts, you'll find stacks of Blue Bird Flour, the cloth-packaged brand favored by Navajo for making fry bread. A counter near the back displays medicinal and ceremonial herbs while another room contains rugs, pottery, and works crafted by regional artists. That's not to say there aren't *some* T-shirts, historical books, flute music CDs, and coffee mugs; there are. But customers are just as likely to plop a bag of Fritos and some aluminum foil in front of the cashier as they are to set down an authentic woven rug.

The Teec Nos Pos Trading Posts sits at the corner of US 64 and US 160. Turn right onto US 160 to go to Four Corners Monument. Although you are in Arizona at this point, you re-enter New Mexico 5 miles down the road, immediately before a white sign with red letters announces your arrival at the Navajo Tribal Park. Make a left turn, and pay the general admission fee of $3/person (children under 6 are free).

Medicinal herbs for sale at the Teec Nos Pos Trading Post

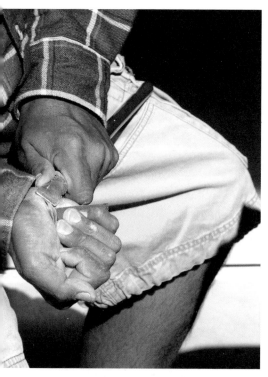

A Navajo craftsman fashions an arrowhead.

Artists and craftsmen sell their wares in the marketplace at Four Corners.

Unlike national parks or even other Navajo tribal parks, Four Corners Monument has few amenities. The Navajo Nation Parks & Recreation recommends that you bring your own "water, food, snacks, hand wipes, and extra toiletries" even though there are a few vendors on site selling fry bread from shacks and trailers. They also point out that the area has no running water, no electricity, and no telephones. Don't expect a visitors center with interpretive exhibits and indoor plumbing either. Porta-Potties line the dirt parking lot, and the "visitor center" is an open-air market with Navajo and Ute vendors selling jewelry, bows, arrows, horsehair pottery, and T-shirts.

Anticipate spending an hour here. Depending on how crowded it is, head first to the monument—a granite and brass circle that marks the point where Arizona, Colorado, New Mexico, and Utah meet. This is the only place in the nation where four states intersect at one point, and it makes for fun photographs, which is part of the problem. At times, hovering people waiting for their own turn inadvertently step into your viewfinder. Instead of fighting the crowds, shop until there's a lull, and then, gather your family and friends for photos.

Turn left as you return to US 160.

Within a mile, you leave New Mexico, enter Colorado, and cross the San Juan River. Ahead, take in the panoramic view of Sleeping Ute Mountain, a peak within the Ute Mountain range. Ute legend describes the mountain as the sleeping form of a Great Warrior God who fell asleep while recovering from wounds received during a battle with the Evil Ones. The blood from his wound turned into water for the animals to drink, and the foliage serves as his blanket. The Ute believe that one day the Great Warrior God will rise again to help them fight their enemies.

Twenty minutes after leaving the Four Corners Monument, US 160 merges with US 491 and continues north to Cortez. You can head south on US 491 back to Shiprock at this point or detour north to Towaoc, the headquarters of the Ute Mountain Ute Indian Reservation. One of only two remaining Native American tribes in Colorado (the other is the Southern Ute Tribe near Durango), the Ute Mountain Utes operate the Ute Mountain Casino, which appears on the left. In addition to 370 slot machines, live blackjack, high-stakes bingo, and live entertainment, the complex includes a hotel, restaurant, RV park, campground, and travel center.

Looking for a Native American collectible? Continue north a mile to Ute

WHO ARE THE UTES?

Just the oldest continuous residents in Colorado. Originally, they inhabited in an area that encompassed all of Colorado, parts of Utah, and the Four Corners region. Today, they've condensed into three bands: the Southern Utes, the Ute Mountain Utes, and the Northern Utes of Utah.

Posing for a photo where the four states meet

Vases for sale at Ute Mountain Indian Pottery

Mountain Indian Pottery. The nondescript shop sits on the right side of the highway under a large yellow sign reading UTE MOUNTAIN POTTERY. Originally known for their intricate beadwork, the tribe formed its pottery enterprise in 1973 and developed a style featuring pastel colors such as sky blue, lavender, and pink. The pottery has become immensely popular over the last four decades. Inside, the shelves hold colorful vases, mugs, cookie jars, piggy banks, and even lampshades. Browse the individually signed pieces, pausing to watch the artists at work on the other side of the glass window in the back of the store.

Ute Mountain Ute Tribal Park offers visitors an opportunity to visit Ancestral Puebloan ruins similar to those found in the adjacent Mesa Verde National Park but without the crowds. Before you go, pack a lunch, bring water, and fill your gas tank, especially if you plan to follow the guide in your own vehicle—the park's 125,000 acres are remote. Then, follow the signs from US 491/US 160 to the visitor center, where you can schedule a half-day, full-day, or private tour with a Ute guide.

As you venture 40 miles into the park's canyons on your tour, you traverse a land still dotted with pottery shards, ancient corn cobs, and primitive tools. On the tour, you will explore pictograph sites, unexcavated ruins, and cliff dwellings. This is a more casual, more personal experience visiting the area's ruins than a visit to nearby Mesa Verde National Park.

The remainder of the drive loops back to Shiprock. Head south on US 491. Watch for Shiprock Pinnacle on the horizon. You'll arrive at the intersection of US 491 and US 64 about a half hour after leaving Towaoc. If you skipped the Ute Mountain Ute Reservation and turned south where the US 160 ended at US 491, your drive to Shiprock should take about 20 minutes.

Since Shiprock has few options for travelers when it comes to dining and accommodations, plan to stay in Farmington, a 30-minute drive to the west on US 64, or in Cortez, 42 miles to the north on US 491. If you do stay in Cortez, you can complete the drive through Canyon of the Ancients, including Mesa Verde National Park. Nearby, Farmington is the endpoint for the drive that includes Chaco Canyon.

Rock art in the Ute Mountain Tribal Park *Matt Inden of Weaver Multimedia Group and the Colorado Tourism Office*

IN THE AREA

ACCOMMODATIONS

Along this route, you'll drive through two cities, Shiprock, New Mexico, and Teec Nos Pos, Arizona; neither has accommodations. The suggested detour north to Towaoc, Colorado, takes you to the Ute Mountain Ute Tribe Reservation and the Ute Mountain Casino, which has a hotel, RV park, and campground. Less than an hour drive north on US 491, Cortez has several hotels, bed & breakfasts, and campgrounds (see the previous chapter for more information). Farmington, 30 miles west on US 64, is another option.

Ute Mountain Casino, US 160, 11 miles south of Cortez, CO. Call 970-565-8800 or 1-800-258-8007. Clean, simple rooms with Anasazi accents. Web site: www.utemountaincasino .com.

Ute Mountain RV Park & Campground, US 160, 11 miles south of Cortez, CO. Call 970-565-9412 or 1-800-889-5072. This campground has both pull through RV and tent spaces. Full hookup is $25.30/night; tent camping is $19/night. Web site: www .utemountaincasino.com/rv_park.html.

ATTRACTIONS AND RECREATION

Four Corners Monument, 6 miles north of Teec Nos Pos. Four states — Arizona, Colorado, New Mexico, and Utah — intersect at this remote point, which has no running water, electricity, or telephones. After the photo ops, stroll the perimeter where artists sell handmade jewelry and crafts. Or, take a 30-minute hike along the Dancin' Horse Trail to the top of the Ute Mountain Lookout Butte. Maps are available to download online from Navajo Nation Parks & Recreation. The park is open daily but hours are seasonal. From May 1 through September 30, the park is open 7 AM–8 PM; the rest of the year, it is open 8 AM-5 PM. General admission is $3/person, free for children 6 and under. Web site: www.navajonation parks.org.

Foutz Trading Company, US 64, Shiprock, NM. Call 505-368-5790 or 1-800-383-0615. The trading post sells rugs, pottery, sand paintings, sculptures, kachinas, and more. Web site: www.foutztrade.com.

Northern Navajo Nation Fair, Shiprock, NM. Call 505-368-5789. The oldest and most traditional of the Navajo fairs, the Shiprock fair is held each fall at the city's fairgrounds, off US 491 at Uranium Boulevard. Admission is charged. The event is held in the fall, usually after the first frost. Web site: www.northernnavajonation fair.org.

Shiprock Pinnacle, Shiprock, NM. A 1,583-foot pinnacle located about 13 miles southwest of the town of Shiprock, so called because some say it resembles a Spanish galleon.

Shiprock Pinnacle is one of the area's best known landmarks.

Teec Nos Pos Trading Post, at the intersection of US 160 and US 64, Teec Nos Pos, AZ. Call 928-656-3224. This isn't your typical trading post stocked with T-shirts, scorpion paperweights, and disposable cameras. Part general store and part gallery, this post showcases the craftsmanship of Navajo, Hopi, Zuni, and Pueblo artists and also sells ceremonial supplies like buckskins and baskets. Web site: www.tnptradingpost.com.

Ute Mountain Indian Pottery, 8 miles south of Cortez on US 160. Call 970-565-8548. Watch as Ute artists at work and then purchase your favorites for souvenirs. Web site: www.utemountainute.com.

Ute Mountain Ute Tribal Park, Towaoc, CO. Call 970-749-1452. Ute guides take visitors on full-day and half-day tours to ancestral Pueblo ruins and cliff dwellings, which are located 42 miles off US 160/491, on dirt and gravel roads. Web site: www.utemountainute.com.

DINING

Dining is very limited along this route. Fast food dominates the restaurant scene in Shiprock with only a few non-chain options avail-

A Native American drum

able. At the Four Corners Monument, Navajo vendors sell fry bread, but you'll have to detour to the Ute Mountain Casino for sit down fare. Or, you may want to continue on into Cortez, Colorado, or Farmington, New Mexico, for more options.

Bamboo Chinese Restaurant, 300 Rural, Shiprock, NM. Call 505-368-3892.

Burger King, US 491, Shiprock, NM. Call 505-368-4801.

Chat & Chew, on 1st Street, south of Indian Route 364, Shiprock, NM. Call 505-368-4875. A local favorite, this small place serves burgers and fries.

KFC, US 491, Shiprock, NM. Call 505-368-4805.

Kuchu's, US 160, 11 miles south of Cortez, CO. Call 970-565-8800 or 1-800-258-8007. The restaurant at Ute Mountain Casino has a limited menu and a cafeteria-style buffet serving daily themes like Mexican and Italian. A breakfast buffet is available on Friday, Saturday, and Sunday. Open Sunday through Thursday, 6 AM–10 PM, and Friday and Saturday, 6 AM–11 PM.

McDonald's, US 491, Shiprock, NM. Call 505-368-3844.

Sonic Drive-In, US 491, Shiprock, NM. Call 505-368-3148.

OTHER CONTACTS

Farmington Convention & Visitors Bureau, 203 W. Main Street, Farmington, NM. Call 505-326-7602. The Farmington Convention & Visitors Bureau covers the Shiprock and Four Corners area as well as Farmington. Web site: www.farmingtonnm.org.

Mesa Verde Country Visitor Information Bureau, Cortez, CO. Call 970-565-8227. The bureau's online resources include maps, itineraries, a calendar, and information on local attractions, lodging, dining, shopping, and more. Web site: www.mesaverde country.com.

Navajo Nation Parks & Recreation, Bldg. 36A at AZ 264 and Indian Route 12, AZ, Window Rock. Call 928-871-6647. The parks and recreation department oversees the Navajo Nation's tribal parks including Four Corners Monument Tribal Park. Find information online about all of the parks, events, permits, and facility rentals. Web site: www.navajonation parks.org.

Navajo Nation Tourism Department. Call 928-871-6436. The tourism department can answer specific questions. For general information, check out DiscoverNavajo.com, the tourism department's online resource. You'll find itineraries, maps, lodging suggestions, and cultural information here. Web site: www.discovernavajo .com.

An inflatable kayak on class II rapids near Durango *Matt Inden of Weaver Multimedia Group and the Colorado Tourism Office*

3 The Riches of the San Juan Mountains

Estimated length: 60 miles to Pagosa Springs
Estimated time: 1.5 hours to Pagosa Springs

Getting there: From Albuquerque, take I-25 north to US 550, Exit 242. Continue on US 550 for approximately 3.5 hours to Durango. From Grand Junction, Colorado, take US 50 south. In Montrose, continue on US 550 South to Durango.

Highlights: In the summer, raft the Animas River in Durango, ride the train to Silverton, fish for trophy trout, and check out the local farms and farmers markets. Then, head to the ruins at Chimney Rock and on to Pagosa Springs. During the winter, snowboard or ski at Purgatory. You can explore the history of the Southern Ute people any time of the year at the Southern Ute Cultural Center.

Humans have inhabited Southern Colorado for more than 10,000 years, lured by abundant water, fertile soil, and animals for hunting. Big game hunters came first, followed by hunter-gatherers who constructed shallow pithouses. Later, Ancestral Puebloans designed multistory villages. Evidence of their presence can be found at nearby Aztec Ruins National Monument and Mesa Verde National Park.

Ute Indians appeared in the Animas Valley as early as the 13th century. At first, they lived as nomadic hunters and gatherers, but with the introduction of horses stolen from the Spanish, they became raiders and traders. Navajo arrived in the area approximately 400 years later.

Then the Anglos came. In 1860, a prospector discovered gold in the San Juan Mountains north of what would later become Durango, and people flooded the region. Through a series of treaties with the U.S. government, ownership of the

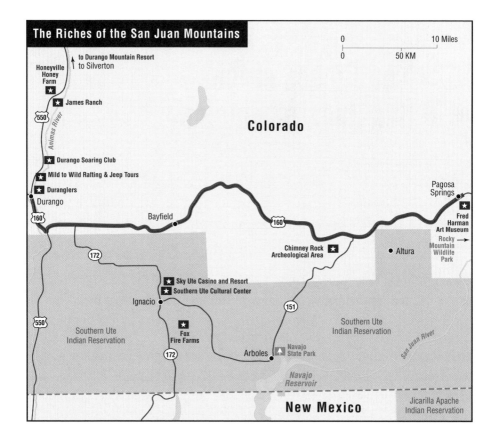

The Riches of the San Juan Mountains

lands was transferred from the Indians to the newcomers. Navajo still in the area wound up on the reservation in Arizona while the Ute people, who once claimed almost all of Colorado for their own, found themselves restricted to reservations near Towaoc and Ignacio.

In September 1881, the Denver and Rio Grande Railroad (D&RG) began serving the San Juan mining district. Railroad officials originally planned to build a station in the existing community of Animas City, but the city refused to pay the railroad dowry, and company executives created their own town nearby, naming it after Durango, Mexico, and Durango, Spain. Durango means "water town" in Spanish.

With such a rich history and bountiful environment, it takes time to explore this part of Southern Colorado, so plan to vacation in Durango and complete the drive as a day trip. Depending on what time of year you go, your time in the Durango area can be a very different experience.

If you go during the summer, enjoy one of the area's most popular activities: rafting. Timing is everything, though. Go too early in the season, and runoff from the San Juan Mountains makes navigating the Animas River a harrowing and icy adventure. On the other hand, if you wait until August, you can step off the river dryer than you would after riding the Grizzly River Run at Disneyland. **Mild to Wild Rafting & Jeep Tours** suggests booking a rafting trip around the Fourth of July for the best experience. Full-day, half-day, and two-hour excursions are typically offered in Durango.

The Animas River also offers world-class fly fishing opportunities with fishermen routinely pulling 10- to 15-inch rainbow and brown trout from its Gold Medal–designated waters. Don't know how to fly fish? Don't worry. Guides like **Duranglers** offer fly-fishing classes in addition to guide services and a full-service fly storefront. If you want to explore regional fishing more, the San Juan, Dolores, and Piedra rivers are all an hour or less from town.

Durango supports its local farms, like James Ranch, which makes its own cheese.

An engineer aboard the Durango Silverton Narrow Gauge Railroad

Other recreational opportunities abound. Hiking, of course, is popular as is mountain biking and horseback riding. For an aerial perspective, though, try gliding. The **Durango Soaring Club** treats passengers to scenic, silent views of the San Juan Mountains and Animas River below. Hot air balloon rides are also available if you're unsure about sailplanes.

During the summer months, experience Durango through its farm-fresh fruits, vegetables, and locally produced artisanal foods. You can tour **James Ranch**, just north of Durango on US 550, and purchase produce from their gardens, beef from their herds, fresh eggs laid by their hens, and cheese made onsite. **Fox Fire Farms** near Ignacio gives visitors a similar experience, but instead of cheese, they sell organic wine from their own vineyards. Across the street from James Ranch,

The Indian Trading Post in Silverton

Honeyville Honey Farm sells locally produced wildflower honey, flavored and whipped honeys, and mead. Sample the lemon whipped honey, chocolate fudge sauce, or any other product by asking the cashier for a taste.

If you happen to be in town on a Saturday morning, head to the First National Bank for the Durango Farmers Market. Held from 8 to 12 in the bank's parking lot, the market includes live music, food vendors, and of course farmers peddling locally grown produce. Get there early if you want fresh eggs, since these sell out quickly.

The railroad literally created Durango in 1881; today, it's the town's main attraction. Purchase tickets online before you go or at the historic 1882 depot in downtown Durango. Although you can ride **Durango & Silverton Narrow Gauge Railroad** (D&SNGRR) both ways to Silverton, consider taking the motor coach there and returning by train, or vice versa. It takes the train 3.5 hours to steam from one end of the line to the other, which severely limits the amount of time you can spend in the tiny mining community at the base of the San Juan Mountains.

I recommend taking the shuttle to Silverton and riding the train back to Durango, instead of the other way around, because the motor coach drivers tell you

HISTORIC RAILROADS OF THE SOUTHWEST

The Durango & Silverton Narrow Gauge Railroad isn't the Four Corners' only historic passenger railroad in Indian Country. The following list provides other options in Indian Country:

❖ **Cripple Creek and Victor Narrow Gauge Railroad,** Cripple Creek, CO. Call 719-689-2640. Although the 4-mile roundtrip excursion on this historic steam engine lasts only 45 minutes, it's also one of the most economical train rides. Tickets cost $13/adults and $8/children 3–12. Web site: www.cripplecreekrailroad.com.

❖ **Cumbres & Toltec Scenic Railroad,** Chama, NM. Call 1-888-286-2737. America's longest and highest narrow-gauge railroad runs 64 miles from Chama to Antonito, Colorado. Take a self-guided tour of the 1881 Chama Yard that includes the depot, roundhouse, and engine shop. Rates range from $75/adults, $40/children 2–12. Web site: www.cumbrestoltec.com.

❖ **Grand Canyon Railway,** 233 N. Grand Canyon Boulevard, Williams, AZ. Call 1-800-843-8724. Ride vintage 1950s and 1970s-era diesel locomotives 65 miles through high desert plains, small arroyos, and portions of the world's largest ponderosa pine forest to the Grand Canyon. Along the way, you'll be entertained by roaming singers and experience an Old Western train robbery. Rates range from $70/adults, $40/children 2–15, plus an $8/person National Park Service entry fee for people 17 and over. Web site: www.thetrain.com.

❖ **Rio Grande Scenic Railroad,** 610 State Street, Alamosa, CO. Call 877-726-7245. Cutting through the San Luis Valley and San Isabel National Forest, this railroad features two cars from the City of New Orleans train, the

about the train, the San Juan Mountains, movies filmed in the area, and what you can expect to see from the railroad on the way home. The train does not provide any narration, allowing you to enjoy the scenery. For me, having the driver's perspective enhanced my train ride back to Durango.

Storefronts and restaurants line Silverton's main streets, Greene and Blair. If you're hungry, grab lunch at **Thee Pitt's Again.** The restaurant, featured on the

Engine 481 of the Durango and Silverton Narrow Guage Railroad
Matt Inden of Weaver Multimedia Group and the Colorado Tourism Office

same one that inspired the famous folk song. Rates begin at $58/adult, $48/child. Club car rates are much higher: $149/adults and $139/children. Web site: www.riograndescenicrailroad.com.

✤ **Royal Gorge Route Railroad,** 401 Water Street, Canon City, CO. Call 1-888-724-5748. Journey 24 miles through the Royal Gorge on a 1950s diesel locomotive. You'll experience breathtaking views and have your choice of five classes of service. Tickets start at $33/person. Web site: www.royal gorgeroute.com.

Food Network show *Diners, Drive-ins and Dives,* serves hearty BBQ sandwiches, ribs, brisket, pulled turkey, and mesquite-smoked salmon. You might also want to visit Montanya Distillers, makers of "award-winning, obsessively crafted high mountain rum." The distillery serves free samples of its two offerings—Platino Light Rum and Oro Dark Rum—and mixes fresh cocktails, like the Sriracha Sour and a rum margarita. Nonalcoholic drinks like Montanya iced chai are also available.

Don't miss the railroad museum at the Durango DSNGRR station.

Whether you decide to ride the train to Silverton, back to Durango, or both ways, you'll be treated to waterfalls, neck-straining mountain views, and trestle bridge crossings on what *National Geographic Traveler* ranks as the number one train rides in North America. Keep an eye out for deer, bears, and other wildlife, and don't worry about what side of the train you're seated on. Both have equally spectacular views. Note: The train makes multiple stops along the way to pick up hikers and, later, zipliners who've spent the day soaring over a mile between 32 platforms at Soaring Tree Top Adventures.

Either before or after your train ride, spend some time in the railroad's museum, located behind the depot. The 12,000-square-foot museum contains steam locomotives, vintage railroad cars, a 1915 American LaFrance fire engine, and a luggage car built as a prop for the movie *Butch Cassidy & the Sundance Kid*. Other items on display include lanterns, keys, railroad signs, and photographs. Near the back a scale model railroad depicts the Denver & Rio Grande Railroad as it would have appeared in the 1950s.

During the winter, the train curtails its schedule, the farmers market shuts down, and summer activities, like rafting and hiking, aren't feasible. Instead, visitors participate in winter sports like skiing, cross-country skiing, ice skating, sledding, ice fishing, showshoeing, snowboarding, and snowmobiling. Purgatory at Durango Mountain Resort is the area's premier winter destination with 88 trails, three terrain parks, and 1,360 skiable acres.

The railroad travels alongside the Animas River towards Silverton.

Before you leave Durango, stroll through the downtown area, shop at the boutique shops, and then drop by the Strater Hotel. Louis L'Amour worked on his Sackett novels in Room 222, where he could take in the ambiance of the saloon below. Music still plays nightly as waitresses dressed in Can-Can outfits take diners' orders. Think the Strater's front desk looks familiar? It should. Clark Griswold robbed the hotel in the movie *National Lampoon's Vacation*.

The drive to Pagosa Springs begins by heading south on US 160/550. Within the first mile, you'll cross the Animas River, and 2 miles down the road, you'll cross it. Look for river rafters below; it's a good distraction from the Coca-Cola bottling facility, box stores, and Durango Mall along the highway. At the edge of town, US 160 splits from US 550. Continue on US 160 to for 3 miles to CO 172. Turn right.

Although a sign indicates you immediately enter the Southern Ute Indian Reservation, that's not necessarily the case. The next 12 miles are a patchwork of reservation and privately owned land with farms and cattle dominating the landscape. Roll down the window during the summer, and you'll likely smell alfalfa and hay.

On the left, the Sky Ute Casino and Resort signals your arrival into Ignacio, the rural community where the Southern Ute tribal council conducts its business. Drive past the casino, through the light, and turn left at the Southern Ute Cul-

The Southern Ute Cultural Center & Museum

The area surrounding Chimney Rock contains 91 Ancestral Puebloan structures.

tural Center & Museum. Of all the museums devoted to a specific Native American tribe, this is by far the best. Plan to spend *at least* an hour touring the interactive exhibits here. Highlights include the 7-screen *Circle of Life* video; recorded retellings of the creation story around a faux campfire; a ghost dance dress; and a traditionally made teepee.

From the cultural center, you can continue south on CO 172 to CO 151, which loops past Navajo State Park and eventually back to US 160 near Chimney Rock. Or you can backtrack the way you came, which puts you about midway between Durango and Bayfield. If you take the latter route, you'll enter the San Juan National Forest and follow Yellow Jacket Creek for a while.

At Milemarker 124, try to spot Chimney Rock on your right side. The treeless peak with a chimney-shaped column should be easy to pick out. Turn right at CO 151 and drive 3 miles to south to the entrance for Chimney Rock Archeological Area. Managed jointly by the United States Forest Service and the Chimney Rock Interpretive Association, the archaeological site has a visitor center and conducts daily walking tours of the Ancestral Puebloan ruins. The guided tours last ap-

HEALING WATERS

Pagosah is the Southern Ute word for "healing waters." According to legend, Ute ancestors experienced a devastating plague, and seeking divine help, they worshipped, prayed, and danced by the San Juan River until they collapsed from exhaustion. When they woke, water had bubbled up from the coals of their ceremonial fires. Thinking it must be a divine sign, they bathed in the water and were cured.

Hot spring soakers relax at the Springs Resort in Pagosa Springs.
Matt Inden of Weaver Multimedia Group and the Colorado Tourism Office

If you visit the hot springs in Pagosa or Durango, keep a few things in mind. First, limit your soaks to approximately 10-minute sessions and drink plenty of fresh water. DO NOT drink the mineral water. Although many local residents and Native Americans drink the hot springs waters, visitors who do so for the first time suffer an "intense purgative effect."

proximately 2.5 hours, but you can take a self-guided tour of the Great Kiva and Great House, if you're on a tight schedule.

Chimney Rock is approximately 20 minutes west of Pagosa Springs. On the way, you'll pass the entrance for Keyah Grande, a $2,000/night lodge that can accommodate up to 20 guests, and farther down, you'll see a sign announcing the headquarters of Parelli Natural Horsemanship, an internationally recognized program that focuses on teaching the human rather than training the horse. Mobile homes are the first sign that you've actually reached Pagosa Springs. Gradually, these give way to A-frame cabins, an RV park, larger homes, and golf courses.

The Pagosa Springs experience is much like that in Durango, minus the train. During the summer, you can raft the San Juan and Piedra rivers, and fish the same rivers Durango guides take their guests to. Mountain biking, hiking, horseback riding, and kayaking are popular, too. Winter activities include skiing, snowboarding, sledding, cross-country skiing, and snowmobiling.

While in Pagosa Springs, visit two of the area's most popular attractions. The Fred Harman Art Museum showcases the work of sculptor, illustrator and *Red Ryder and Little Beaver* cartoonist, Fred Harman, while just outside of town, on US 84, the Rocky Mountain Wildlife Park provides homes for wild animals that cannot live in the wild on their own. Afternoon feeding tours of the wildlife park are available daily as well as trail rides through Lobo Outfitters.

Allow several days, if not a week, to explore the San Juan Mountains, Durango, Pagosa Springs and the Southern Ute Indian Reservation. You'll find this is a trip you don't want to end.

IN THE AREA

ACCOMMODATIONS

Durango Mountain Resort, #1 Skier Place, Durango. Call 970-247-9000. The resort offers more than lodging. During the winter, you can ski Purgatory's 88 trails, snowboard, cross-country ski, and participate in other winter sports. Things don't slow down when the snow melts. Summer activities include ziplining, mountain biking, an alpine slide, miniature golf, and bungee jumping. Call for rates and package deals. Web site: www .durangomountainresort.com.

Pass Creek Yurt, Pagosa Springs. Call 970-731-2486. Stay in a yurt near the Continental Divide. The 20-foot space sleeps six and makes a great base for mountain biking, hiking, and fishing. Web site: www.wolfcreekbackcountry .com.

Healing Waters Resort & Spa, 317 Hot Springs Boulevard, Pagosa Springs. Call 970-264-5910 or 1-800-832-5523. Rooms at this resort come with access to the hot springs, where you'll enjoy a hot mineral pool, outdoor soaking tub, and indoor baths. The spa offers standard massages like Swedish, therapeutic, and shiatsu. Room rates from $75 to $250/night. Even if you don't stay at the resort, you can enjoy the hot mineral pool for a fee: $10/ages 13–64, $8/seniors, and $7/children 3–12. Web site: www.pshotsprings.com.

Sky Ute Casino Resort, 14324 US 172, Ignacio. Call 970-563-7777. Opened in November 2008, the resort has 130 guest rooms, four restaurants, a convention center and, of course, a casino. Additional attractions include a lazy river indoor swimming pool, miniature golf, an arcade, and a bowling alley. Room rates from $80/night up to $300/night. Web site: www.sky utecasino.com.

The Springs Resort & Spa, 165 Hot Springs Boulevard, Pagosa Springs. Call 1-800-225-0934. Although it is a resort, it's better known for its 17 therapeutic hot spring pools and a Mediterranean-style bathhouse that are open to the public. Room rates from $289/night. Web site: www .pagosahotsprings.com.

Strater Hotel, 699 Main Avenue, Durango. Call 970-247-4431 or 1-800-247-4431. A National Historic Landmark, the Strater Hotel's 93 rooms feature hand-stenciled wall-papers and antiques. The Western ambiance inspired writer Louis L'Amour, who worked on his Sackett novels in Room 222, directly above the saloon. Web site: www.strater.com.

Westerly RV Park, 6440 County Road 203, Durango. Call 970-247-1275. Located 5 miles north of Durango, this 26-site park has full-hook-ups and discounted access to Trimble Hot Springs across the street. Web site: www.westerlyrvpark.com.

ATTRACTIONS AND RECREATION

Chimney Rock Archeological Area, located 3 miles south of US 160 on CO 151, Pagosa Springs. Call 970-883-5359. Home to Ancestral Puebloan people, the Chimney Rock area contains 91 structures and 27 outlying camps, for a total of more than 200 rooms. Begin your visit at the Visitor Center Cabin, which includes a pithouse model and artifact displays. You can take a self-guided walking tour of the Great Kiva and the Great House daily between 10:30 and 2:30, or take a guided tour at 9:30, 10:30, 1, and 2. The visitor center is open May 15 through September 30, daily 9–4:30. Entrance is $10/adults and $5/children 5–11. Web site: www .chimneyrockco.org.

Durango & Silverton Narrow Gauge Railroad and Museum, 479 Main Avenue, Durango. Call 970-247-2733. Climb aboard a 1880s-era steam locomotive for a 3.5-hour, 45-mile journey from Durango to Silverton along the Animas River. If you don't have time for the train ride, you can still visit the railroad's museum, located at the south end of the roundhouse in Durango. Or, take a yard tour, held daily at 10:30 and 2:30, May through October. Admission to the museums is free; there's a $10/adult and $5/child fee for the yard tour ($5/adult and $2.50/child with train ticket). Coach fare for train is $83/ages 12 and over and $49/children 4–11, plus 4 percent historic preservation fee. Web site: www.durangotrain.com.

Durango Soaring Club, 27290 US 550, Durango. Call 970-247-9037. On a clear day, you can see 100 miles in any direction as you glide in a sailplane over the San Juan Mountains and Animas River. Rates begin at $100 for 20 minutes. Web site: www.soardurango.com.

Fox Fire Farms, 5733 County Road 321, Ignacio. Call 970-563-4675. Kids will love visiting Fox Fire Farms, where they can see how food gets from the farm to their table and observe pet baby goats, calves, and more. Adults will enjoy the organic vineyards and sampling local wines. Tours leave daily at 10 and 4 (no morning tours on Saturday or Sunday) and must be booked at least 24 hours in advance. Fee: $20/adults and

$10/children ages 2–16. Web site: www.foxfirefarms.com.

Fred Harman Art Museum, 85 Harman Park Drive, Pagosa Springs. Call 970-731-5785. An established sculptor and illustrator, Fred Harman also created the *Red Ryder and Little Beaver* cartoon strip. The museum displays his original artwork as well as rodeo, movie, and Western memorabilia. Web site: www.harmanartmuseum.com.

Honeyville Honey Farm, 33633 US 550, Durango. Call 970-247-1474 or 1-800-676-7690. Purchase locally produced wildflower honey, flavored and whipped honeys, mead, and other specialty items. Web site: www.honeyvillecolorado.com.

James Ranch, 33846 US 550, Durango. Call 970-385-6858 or 970-247-8652. The ranch offers two touring options. The two-hour electric cart tour allows you to see the seasonal dairy and cheese making facility, visit the gardens, and learn about sustainable farming. A three-hour twilight option includes dinner. Tours run May 1 through September 15. Cost is $18/person for the daytime tour offered Tuesdays and Thursdays at 1 and 3, and $50/person for the dinner tour offered on Wednesday and Saturday. Reservations are required. The ranch also has a market which is open daily 11-6. Web site: www.jamesranch.net.

Mild to Wild Rafting & Jeep Tours, 50 Animas View Drive, Durango. Call 1-800-567-6745. Pick the adventure that suits you, from family-oriented experiences to adrenaline-pumping rapids. Jeep tours and train packages are also available, too. www.mild2wild rafting.com

Montanya Distillers, 1332 Blair Street, Silverton. Call 970-799-3206. Sample the distillery's Platino Light Rum and Oro Dark Rum, purchase your favorite to take home and then order a cocktail. Mixologists create new recipes every week and offer favorites like the lavender blackberry mojito. Nonalcoholic versions are also available. Open daily 11:30–7. Web site: www.montanyadistillers.com.

Rocky Mountain Wildlife Park, 4821A US 84, Pagosa Springs. Call 970-264-5546. This privately owned facility cares for animals that cannot live in the wild on their own. Open May 15 through November 15, daily 9–6. The rest of the year, November 16 through May 14, the park is open 10–4. Tour fees are $7/adults, $6/seniors, and $5/children ages 3–12. You can also schedule one-hour, two-hour, half-day, and full-day trail rides through Lobo Outfitters here. Trail ride rates begin at $30 for one hour. Web site: www.rmwildlifepark.org.

Soaring Tree Top Adventures, Durango. Call 970-769-2357. You'll have to ride the train to get there, but from then on, you'll be soaring as you zi-pline between 32 platforms. Spans range from 56 to 1,400 feet. Costs, including train ticket, begin at $439/person. Web site: www.soaring colorado.com.

Southern Ute Cultural Center & Museum, Ignacio. Call 970-563-9583. Explore the culture and history of the Southern Ute Indian Tribe at this 52,000-square foot, child-friendly facility. Guided tours led by tribal members are available. The museum is open Tuesday through Friday, 10–6; Saturday, 10–4; Sunday, 1–5. Admission is $7/adults, $4/seniors, and $3/children ages 3–14. Web site: www .succm.org.

DINING

Alley House Grille, 214 Pagosa Street, Pagosa Springs. Call 970-264-0999. Chefs Todd and Kellie Stevens create upscale, gourmet dishes. Web site: www.alleyhousegrille.com.

Bar D Chuckwagon Suppers, 8080 County Road 250, Durango. Call 970-247-5753. The Bar D Wranglers entertain after a meal of barbecue roast beef, chicken, or steak served with foil-wrapped potatoes, oven-baked beans, homemade biscuits, apple sauce, and old-fashioned spice cake. Open nightly for dinner, Memorial Day weekend through Labor Day weekend. Reservations required. Web site: www.bardchuckwagon.com.

Linda's Local Food Café, Durango. Call 970-259-6729. Owner Linda Illsley is committed to helping local farmers, so much so that she has adapted her menu to what is available seasonally. Lettuce is out of season? No salads. The hens aren't laying eggs? No eggs. She won't buy from the supermarket across the parking lot. And don't even think about asking for a Diet Coke. Web site: www.cocinalindaonline.com.

Seasons Rotisserie & Grill, 764 Main Avenue, Durango. Call 970-382-9790. Featuring a wood-burning grill and rotisserie, Seasons uses fresh ingredients to create simple but flavorful dishes. Web site: www.seasonsof durango.com.

Steamworks, 801 E. 2nd Avenue, Durango. Call 970-259-9200. There will probably be a wait at this see-and-be-seen brewpub, but don't let it detour you—the food is great, and the beer is even better. Try the Cajun boil, a mix of spicy crab, shrimp, potatoes, corn, and Andouille sausage on newspapers. Wash it down with Steam Engine Lager. Web site: www.steamworksbrewing.com.

Thee Pitt's Again, 1157 Greene Street, Silverton. Call 970-387-5027. Although Guy Fieri's *Diners, Drive-ins and Dives* visited the restaurant's Glendale, Arizona, location, the Silverton location delivers the same mesquite-smoked, Southern-style BBQ. Web site: www.theepittsagain.com.

OTHER CONTACTS

Durango Area Tourism Office, 111 S. Camino Del Rio, Durango. Call 970-247-3500. Find all the information you need to plan a Durango vacation. Web site: www.durango.org.

Pagosa Springs Chamber of Commerce, Pagosa Springs. Call 970-264-2360 or 1-800-252-2204. Web site: www.pagosachamber.com.

Pagosa Springs Dining Guide, 422 Pagosa Street, Pagosa Springs. Call 970-264-4237. This publication offers an interactive online guide. Also online are coupons, maps, and menus. Web site: www.pagosaspringsdining .com.

Pagosa Springs Tourism. Call 800-252-2204. Learn where to stay, where to eat, and what to do. Help is also available for planning events and vacations. Web site: www.visitpagosa springs.com.

San Juan National Forest, U.S. Forest Service, 15 Burnett Court, Durango. Call 970-247-4874. Web site: www.fs .usda.gov/sanjuan.

Southern Ute Indian Tribe, Ignacio. Call 970-563-0100. The tribal Web site has information on visiting the reservation as well as the Southern Ute's culture and history. Web site: www.southern-ute.nsn.us.

The Chacoan great house, Hungo Pavi, at Chaco Culture National Historical Park

4 The Ancestral Puebloans of New Mexico

Estimated length: 165 miles to Farmington

Estimated time: 3 hours to Farmington

Getting there: From Albuquerque, drive north on I-25 for 15 miles to US 550, Exit 242.

Highlights: Heading from Albuquerque toward the Four Corners region, you will drive through six reservations: Santa Ana, Laguna, Zia, Jemez, Navajo, and Jicarilla Apache. The half-hour drive to Chaco Canyon rewards with access to the palatial, multistory ruins of the Ancestral Puebloans. You can also venture into the De-Na-Zin Wilderness and Bisti Badlands, and in the neighboring communities of Bloomfield, Aztec, and Farmington, you'll find more Ancestral Puebloan ruins, trading posts, and museums.

Originally, I titled this chapter "New Mexico's Badlands," after the Bisti Badlands this drive cuts through, since as you travel you'll pass through a very barren and harsh landscape. It's hard to imagine any culture living here, let alone thriving here. But I changed the title to "The Ancestral Puebloans of New Mexico," because these ancient people not only survived, but they created a network of villages, branching out from Chaco Canyon.

Start by exiting I-25 and heading northwest on US 550 toward Farmington. As you enter Bernalillo, you'll cross the Rio Grande River. **Coronado State Monument** is on your right side. Named for Francisco Vasquez de Coronado, who reportedly camped here in 1540, this state monument includes the partially reconstructed ruins of Pueblo Kuaua.

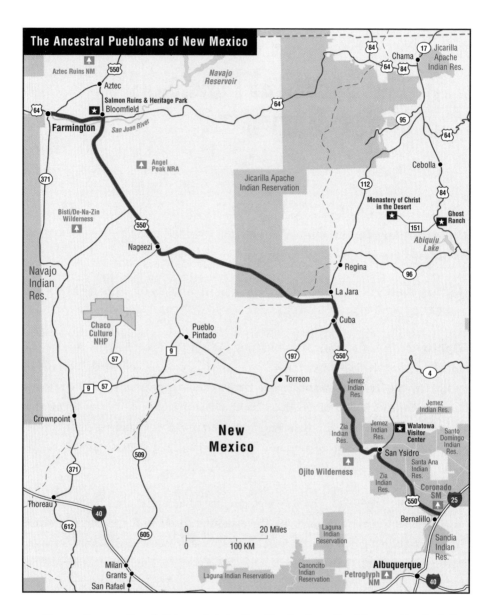

The Ancestral Puebloans of New Mexico

Ten miles north of this point is the Santa Ana Pueblo, a site that the Tamayame people have occupied since the late 1500s. During June and July, they open the pueblo to the public for performances of the Corn Dance, but you can experience Tamayame hospitality year-round by visiting the **Hyatt Regency Tamaya**. Located about a mile behind the tribe's casino on Tamaya Boulevard, the resort offers its guests Tamayame bread making classes, Native American dance demonstrations, tribal-approved spa treatments, storytelling, and regionally inspired food.

Even if you don't stay overnight, you can visit the resort's onsite cultural learning center, which displays traditional clothing from the Tamayames' feast days, old photographs, and exhibits relating to the pueblo's patron saint, St. Anne. Or, you can take a self-guided tour of the Native American artwork on display in the resort's public areas.

Leaving Bernalillo, you enter the Zia (*Zee-ah*) Indian Reservation. Although you can't see the pueblo from the highway, you may be more familiar with Zia than you realize—the red insignia on the New Mexico state flag is the Zia sun symbol and signifies friendship among different cultures. The pueblo opens to the public in August for the feast day of Our Lady of the Assumption.

You can't miss White Mesa on the left as you approach San Ysidro. Colored by gypsum, a mineral commonly used in cement, the mesa is popular with mountain bikers and, to a lesser extent, hikers. To the west of White Mesa, the Ojito Wilderness offers hiking, backpacking, and horseback riding. Remote camping

The road to Chaco Canyon

is also available. Note: this is a dry, arid region with no facilities, so be sure to bring plenty of water, especially if you plan to do any physical activities.

Two miles past White Mesa, you'll find the small farming community of San Ysidro. Founded in 1699 when Juan Trujillo established a settlement for Saint Isidore the Farmer, the community serves as a gateway for the **Jemez Mountain Trail Scenic Byway**, which stretches from San Ysidro in two directions: north on US 550 to Cuba and east on NM 4 to White Rock and Bandelier National Monument. Take a short detour here by turning right on NM 4 and continuing 4 miles to the Jemez (*Hay-mess* or *He-mish*) Pueblo.

Because the Jemez Pueblo shuns the crowds associated with feasts, the tribe doesn't publish their feast dates, but if you are lucky enough to be there at the right time, you are welcome to watch the dances and festivities. As with any pueblo, photographs, weapons, alcohol, and drugs are not permitted. Pets are also not allowed at Jemez Pueblo. For those interested in learning more about the Jemez people and exploring the surrounding area, the tribe maintains the **Walatowa Visitor Center**, where you'll find a museum of history and culture as well as a replica fieldhouse. You can also arrange for tours through the visitor center or a 1.5-mile hike of the Red Rock Canyon Trail for $5/person.

If you want to explore more of the eastern arm of the Jemez Mountain Trail, there's plenty to see. The family-owned **Ponderosa Winery** is located 3 miles off NM 4 on NM 290 and is open Tuesday through Sunday for tastings. Twelve miles past Jemez Pueblo, Jemez Springs beckons with its vintage bath house, hot springs, and Soda Dam, a travertine geological formation. Nearby, Jemez State Monument features 600-year-old Jemez ruins and a 17th-century Spanish mission with an octagonal-shaped bell tower.

This route takes you all the way to NM 502 and US 84, north of Santa Fe, passing the Ancestral Puebloan ruins of Bandelier National Monument. Unless you plan to extend your adventure through this area over several days, though, stick to the original drive, detouring only the few miles to Jemez Pueblo.

Returning to US 550, turn right and head north. As you zigzag through the edges of the Jemez and Zia reservations, you'll notice the sandstone giving way to a flat, grassy expanse. By Milemarker 58, you've entered pine country, and the residences of Cuba come into view. Located at the base of the Nacimiento Mountain Range, this small community is one of the few opportunities you have to fill your gas tank or your stomach for the next 90 miles.

At Milemarker 77, you cross the Continental Divide, and a mile later, you enter the Jicarilla Apache Nation. The Jicarilla (*Hek-a-reh-ya*) originally migrated from Canada between 1300 and 1500 A.D. and settled in a 50-million-acre area that stretched across northern New Mexico, Southern Colorado and western Oklahoma. Today, they occupy roughly 1,400 acres in northern New Mexico. Annual events like the Little Beaver Pow-Wow are open to the general public. Check online or with the tribe directly for more information on dates and accessibility.

ALLIES

The Jicarilla were the only Apaches to join their neighbors in the Pueblo Revolt of 1680.

Unlike other tribes, the Jicarilla haven't fully embraced tourism. They operate the 200-machine Apache Nugget Casino, at Milemarker 85 but much of their economy is based instead on oil, gas, and mining interests.

You begin to sense the remoteness of this land as you drive through the reser-

The 9-mile loop through Chaco Canyon takes you past six major sites.

A dog protects sheep along the road to Chaco Canyon.

vation. In fact, you may even get a little excited when the natural gas processing plant at Lybrook comes into view—at least it's something to look at other than dry desert grasses and shrubs. Fortunately, the turnoff for **Chaco Culture National Historical Park** is only a few miles down the road.

Watch for the Red Mesa Express, a white convenience store with a red roof and gas pumps, at Milemarker 102.5. Chaco Canyon doesn't have gas or concessions, so at the very least, you'll want to stock up on water and snacks. Turn back onto US 550. The sign for Chaco Canyon is just north of the convenience store and directs you to turn left onto County Road 7900. Although this portion of the road is paved, when you turn right onto County Road 7950 to continue to Chaco Canyon (driving straight takes you to Pueblo Pintado), the road becomes a teeth-jarring test of endurance. I live on a dirt road, and I agree with the National Park

Service, that CR 7950 is "rough." That said, I didn't have a problem driving it in my Dodge Charger. It was just slow going. Expect it to take 30-45 minutes to reach the visitor center, where you'll pay the park entrance fee.

Budget at least three hours to see the park in its entirety, especially if you intend to take the free, ranger-led tours. From the visitor center, turn right and make your way along the 9-mile, one-way park loop. You probably noticed Fajada Butte before (ahead and a little to the left as you leave the visitor center), but it's worth a second glance now. Three rock slabs and two spiral petroglyphs seem to have functioned as a solstice marker for the people living in Chaco Canyon. In an effort to preserve the area, access to Fajada is restricted.

The first stop is Hungo Pavi at the mouth of Mockingbird Canyon. If you have time, stop. Otherwise, skip ahead to Chetro Ketl. This Ancestral Puebloan site features 500 rooms and 16 kivas, but that's nothing compared to its neighbor, Pueblo Bonito. Inhabited from the mid-800s to 1200s, this structure once towered four stories high and included more than 600 rooms and 40 kivas. For an impressive view, take the PuebloAlto Trail to the Pueblo Bonito Overlook, a one-hour, 2-mile hike roundtrip.

At the end of the loop, Pueblo del Arroyo features a plaza and a tri-wall structure that is rare for the Chaco region. Look for the Pueblo Alto Trailhead near the parking area. In addition to the Pueblo Bonito Overlook, this 5.4-mile loop trail passes by Chacoan stairways, ramps, and roads. You can also access the 7.4-mile Penasco Blanco Trail from the Pueblo Del Arroyo parking lot. This trail

THE BACK, BACKROADS OF CHACO CANYON

Maps show several routes into Chaco Culture National Historical Park, but the main route and the one recommended by this book is County Road 7900 from US 550. If you are going to attempt another route, call the National Park Service (505-786-7014) first to verify road conditions and vehicle requirements. Do not set out on these alternative routes in an RV.

Also, several visitors have reported that their Global Positioning System (GPS) devices are not accurate in the area. Rely on written directions and printed maps to make your way to Chaco Canyon.

Pueblo Bonito once stood four stories high and included more than 600 rooms.

takes hikers past the Kin Kletso, Casa Chiquita, and Penasco Blanco ruins, plus petroglyphs and pictographs. You will need a hiking permit from the visitor center, plenty of water, and sunscreen.

Casa Rinconada completes the Chaco Canyon loop. At this site, you'll see the largest known Great Kiva in the park. There's also a trailhead here that leads to the great house of Tsin Kletzin.

Fifteen miles after returning to US 550, you can access the 45,000-acre Bisti/De-Na-Zin Wilderness by taking County Road 7500 west. Since motorized vehicles and mountain bikes are prohibited in the Bisti (*Bis-tie*) and De-Na-Zin (*Deh-nah-zin*) areas, you will have to park at designated lots and hike to see the mushroom-shaped hoodoos, spires, petroglyphs, and fossils that make this desolate region so unique. Again, bring plenty of water and wear sunscreen.

The barren areas off US 550 are gradually replaced by farm fields as you approach Bloomfield. Although this community was established in 1879, prehistoric farmers began planting in the area as early as the 11th century. You can see evidence of these people at the **Salmon Ruins & Heritage Park** in Bloomfield. To get to the ruins, turn left at US 64 and head toward Farmington. In addition to a Chacoan great house, you'll find a 19th-century homestead and replicas of a sweatlodge, hogan, tipi, and pithouse.

Aztec Ruins National Monument is also in the area, although you'll have to continue north on US 550 to get there and backtrack to US 64 to reach Farmington. The side trip is worth it. The Ancestral Puebloan great house at this monument has more than 500 rooms and boasts the nation's largest reconstructed kiva.

US 64 brings you to Farmington, an agricultural and oil-refining community on the San Juan and Animas rivers. You could spend several days in town rafting the Animas River, strolling along the River Walk, fishing the San Juan River, visiting the **E3 Children's Museum & Science Center,** and exploring the **Farm-**

You'll see kivas like this one at Chaco Culture National Historical Park.

ington Museum at Gateway Park. Or you could tour B-Square Ranch, a 12,000-acre wildlife refuge with two museums, the Bolack Museum of Fish and Wildlife and the Bolak Electromechanical Museum.

Navajo travel from the nearby reservation to exchange or sell their crafts in Farmington. The city has three trading posts: Fifth Generation Trading Company, Shiprock Trading Company, and Navajo Trading Company. West of town, halfway between Farmington and Shiprock, you'll find several more, including Hogback Trading Company. Although more expensive than buying directly from the artists, trading posts offer a much wider variety and some prize-winners from regional fairs.

From Farmington, you can easily pick up three other drives. Shiprock is less than 30 miles west and serves as the starting point for the Four Corners Loop. Cortez and Mesa Verde National Park is an 1.5-hour drive north. And Durango is 55 miles to the east.

ALTERNATE ROUTE

D riving north from I-40 at Thoreau—pronounced *thuh-roo* like *threw,* not like *throw*—provides a similar experience. Just north of this one-time railroad town, on NM 371, the route is a scenic mix of red mesas and rural communities that are gradually replaced by desert plains and eventually badlands. Crownpoint, the site of the Crownpoint Navajo Rug Auction, marks the first major community along the drive. The cash-only auction is held the second Friday of the month. Viewing begins at 4, the auction at 6.

You can access Chaco Canyon by taking NM 57 into the park, but the National Park Service labels this route "very rough" compared to the "rough" dirt road off US 550. It also warns that RVs should not attempt NM 57, and at times the road can be impassable. North of Lake Valley, you can also pick up County Road 7750, weave along the sandy and rutted roads to NM 57, and enter the park from that point. This route takes four-wheel drive. Definitely contact the park service for directions and road conditions before attempting.

The Bisti/De-Na-Zin Wilderness Area can be accessed at County Road 7297, about 45 miles north of Crownpoint.

IN THE AREA

ACCOMMODATIONS

Casa Blanca Inn, 505 E. La Plata Street, Farmington. Call 1-800-550-6503. This bed & breakfast provides a complimentary Southwestern-style breakfast buffet and individual patios with courtyard or garden views. Rooms from $130/night. Web site: www.4cornersbandb.com.

Courtyard by Marriott Farmington, 560 Scott Avenue, Farmington. Call 505-325-5111. Web site: www.marriott.com/hotels/travel/fmncy-courtyard-farmington.

Hampton Inn & Suites Farmington, 1500 Bloomfield Boulevard, Farmington. Call 505-564-3100. Overnight stay includes complimentary hot breakfast and free high-speed Internet access. Web site: www.hamptoninn.hilton.com.

Holiday Inn Express Farmington, 2110 Bloomfield Boulevard, Farmington. Call 505-325-2545. Enjoy free high-speed Internet access, a complimentary hot breakfast, and the indoor pool. Rooms from $117/night.

Kokopelli Cave Bed and Breakfast, 5001 Antelope Junction, Farmington. You'll walk down a sloping path and steps cut into sandstone to enter this bed & breakfast, carved into a 65-million-year-old sandstone formation. Kokopelli Cave features plush carpeting, Southwestern furniture, hot and cold running water, a flagstone hot tub and a cascading waterfall-style shower. Rates: $220–260/night.

The Region Inn, 601 E. Broadway, Farmington. Call 505-325-1191 or 1-888-325-1191. Standard, clean rooms from $82/night.

Silver River Adobe Inn, 3151 W. Main Street, Farmington. Call 505-325-8219. Overlooking the confluence of the San Juan and La Plata rivers, the Silver River Adobe Inn is a bed & breakfast with private baths and entrances. After an organic breakfast, schedule a massage with co-owner Diana Ohlson, a licensed massage therapist. Rooms begin at $105/night.

ATTRACTIONS AND RECREATION

Aztec Ruins National Monument, #84 County Road 2900, Aztec. Call 505-334-6174. Located exactly halfway between Chaco Canyon and Mesa Verde, this Ancestral Puebloan ruin is the third-largest great house community, behind Pueblo Bonito and Chetro Ketl in Chaco Canyon. Web site: www.nps.gov/azru.

B-Square Ranch, 3901 Bloomfield Highway, Farmington. Call 505-325-4275. A working farm and ranch, this destination is also a 12,000-acre wildlife refuge and the home of two museums, the Bolack Museum of Fish and Wildlife and the Bolack Electromechanical Museum. Open Monday through Saturday, 9–3. Web site: www.bolackmuseums.com.

Bisti/De-Na-Zin Wilderness, 30 miles south of Farmington. Call 505-599-8900. The eroded badlands of the Bisti and De-Na-Zin wildernesses offer a dramatic landscape that during the late Cretaceous period was populated by dinosaurs, primitive mammals, reptiles, birds, and fish. Hike, mountain bike, backpack, horseback ride, and camp in these 38,305 acres located about 30 miles south of Farmington. There is no fee, but there are also no services. Bring plenty of water. Web site: www.blm.gov/nm/st/en/prog/wilderness/bisti.html.

Chaco Culture National Historical Park, US 550, Nageezi. Call 505-786-7014. Visit Ancestral Puebloan ruins at six major sites. The park offers ranger-guided tours, or you can navigate the self-guided tour along the 9-mile Canyon Loop Drive. Backcountry hiking trails take you to more remote areas, but you will need to obtain a free permit from the visitor center. Open daily 7 AM to sunset. The visitor center is open daily 8–5. The entrance fee is $8/vehicle. Web site: www.nps.gov/chcu. Highlights at the park include:

❖ **Casa Rinconada:** This site has the largest known Great Kiva in the park.

❖ **Chetro Ketl:** Construction on this 500-room structure began around 1020 A.D.

❖ **Fajada Butte:** Rock slabs on the butte seem to have functioned as a solstice marker for the Ancient Puebloans living here.

❖ **Pueblo Bonito:** The center of Cha-coan civilization, this village once consisted of more than 600 rooms and 40 kivas.

❖ **Pueblo del Arroyo:** Partially eroded by the river, this site has a unique, tri-walled structure.

Coronado State Monument, US 550 to Kuaua Road, Bernalillo. Call 505-476-1150. You'll see the partially reconstructed ruins of Pueblo Kuaua. Francisco Vasquez de Coronado is said to have camped near this site with his soldiers in 1540 while searching for the fabled Cities of Gold. Open Wednesday through Monday, 8:30–5. Closed Tuesday. Admission is $3, free for children 16 and under.

Farmington Museum at Gateway Park, 3041 E. Main Street, Farmington. Call 505-599-1174. Exhibits on dinosaurs, oil, farming, and the Three Waters Trading Post. Open Monday through Saturday, 8–5. Admission is free.

Fifth Generation Trading Company, 232 W. Broadway, Farmington. Call 505-326-3211. Seth Benjamin Tanner opened this trading post, also known as the Southwest Showroom, in 1875. In addition to rugs, jewelry, and pottery, Fifth Generation Trading Company boasts the largest collection of Navajo sandpainting art in the Southwest. Web site: www.southwest-showroom.com.

Navajo Trading Company, 126 E. Main Street, Farmington. Call 505-325-1685.

The Bisti Wilderness *New Mexico Tourism Department and James Orr*

Ponderosa Winery, 3171 Hwy. 290, Ponderosa. Call 1-800-946-3657. Situated 5,800 above sea level on volcanic ash deposits, this winery produces award-winning sangiovese, sauvignon blanc, Riesling, and blends. Open Tuesday through Saturday, 10–5, and Sunday, 12–5. Web site: www .ponderosawinery.com.

Riverside Nature Center, located at Animas Park off Browning Parkway, Farmington. Call 505-599-1422. Overlooking the wetlands along the Animas River, the nature center provides wildlife viewing opportunities and trails. Hours vary by season.

Salmon Ruins & Heritage Park, 6131 US 64, Bloomfield. Call 505-632-2013. Explore 11th-century ruins, a Chacoan great house, and a 19th-century homestead. Highlights include a sweatlodge, hogan, tipi, and pithouse. Open Monday through Friday, 9–5; weekends according to the season. Admission is $3/adults, $2/seniors and $1/children 6–16. Web site: www.salmonruins.com.

Shiprock Trading Post, 301 W. Main Street, Farmington. Call 505-324-0881. Established in 1894, this post sells Navajo rugs, jewelry, pottery, baskets, and more. Open Monday through Friday, 9:30–5, and Saturday, 10–4. Web site: www.shiprocktrading post.com.

Walatowa Visitor Center, 7413 NM 4, Jemez Pueblo. Call (575) 834-7235. The visitor center has a museum of history and culture, replica field-house, and a gift shop. Arrange for scenic hikes and other guided tours here. Open daily 8–5. Web site: www .jemezpueblo.com.

White Mesa and Ojito Wilderness, Cabezon Road/County Road 906. Call 505-761-8700. Once covered by an-cient waters, the mesa and wilder-ness area offer outstanding mountain bike and hiking trails. No fees. No fa-cilities.

DINING

3 Rivers Eatery & Brewhouse, 101 E. Main Street, Farmington. Call 505-324-2187. Located in the building that once housed the Farmington Drug Store and the *Farmington Times-Hustler* newspaper, this restaurant and brewery serves pizza, sandwiches, steak, chicken, fish, and of course fresh-brewed beer. Don't miss the 3 Rivers beer label and beer coaster collections, the self-proclaimed largest collection in New Mexico. Web site: www.threeriversbrewery.com.

Bernardone's Family Pizzeria, 933 W. Main Street, Farmington. Call 505-325-0303. Ironically, pizza isn't this restaurant's claim to fame—it's the Italian dishes based on family recipes.

Try the lasagna al forno, chicken parmigiana, or farfalle rustica. The Bernardones also serve hearty cal-zones and sandwiches. Web site: www.bernardonesfamilypizzeria.com.

Blue Moon Diner, 1819 E. 20th Street, Farmington. Call 505-324-0001. The diner dishes up reasonably priced sandwiches, salads, homemade ice cream, and more. Web site: www.blue moon-diner.com.

St. Clair Winery and Bistro, 5150 E. Main Street, Farmington. Call 505-325-0711. One of St. Clair Winery's three bistros, this location pairs French country dishes with award-winning New Mexico wines. Live jazz music plays Thursday through Sun-day. Open daily for lunch and dinner. Web site: www.stclairwinery.com.

Si Señor, 4015 E. 30th Street, Farm-ington. Call 505-324-9050. A favorite with locals, this Mexican restaurant offers south-of-the-border staples like burritos, tamales, and enchiladas.

OTHER CONTACTS

Bureau of Land Management, Rio Puerco Field Office, 435 Montano NE, Albuquerque. Call 505-761-8700.

CubaNewMexico.com. Call 505-289-2222. Web site: www.cubanewmexico .com.

Farmington Convention & Visitors Bureau, 3041 E. Main Street, Farm-ington. Call 505-326-7602. Web site: www.farmingtonnm.org.

Jemez Mountain Trail Scenic Byway. This byway begins just east of Cuba, heads south to San Ysidro, and continues on NM 4 to White Rock. Web site: www.jemezmountaintrail.org.

Jicarilla Apache Nation. Call 575-759-3242. The Jicarilla Apache Nation site provides information on tribal events like powwows and rodeos. Web site: www.jicarillaonline.com.

Pueblo of Santa Ana, 2 Dove Road. Call 505-771-6700. History and tribal information. Web site: www.santaana .org.

Native American artists and craftsmen outside the Palace of the Governors

5 The Pueblos of the Old Spanish Trail

Estimated length: 105 miles to Chama

Estimated time: 2 hours to Chama

Getting there: From Albuquerque, head north on I-25 approximately 60 miles to Exit 282B, St. Francis Drive/US 84.

Highlights: After exploring Santa Fe, you'll head north along the Old Spanish Trail through the pueblos of Tesuque, Pojoaque, Nambe, San Ildefonso, Santa Clara, and Ohkay Owingeh. In Abiquiu, discover the landscapes that inspired artist George O'Keeffe, learn about dinosaurs at Ghost Ranch, and visit a Benedictine monastery. Your journey ends in Chama, where you can board the historic Cumbres & Toltec Scenic Railroad and enjoy spectacular views of the San Juan Mountains.

Based on a loose connection of Native American footpaths, the main route of the Old Spanish Trail cuts north from Santa Fe to avoid the Grand Canyon and continues through Colorado and Utah before swinging south to Los Angeles. The Spanish first explored it in the 1500s, but it wasn't widely used in its entirety until 1829, when Mexican traders led pack mules across its rushing rivers, deep canyons, arid deserts, and towering mountains. Today, by following US 84, you can retrace the general route from Santa Fe to Cebolla through the predominately Tewa-speaking tribes of northern New Mexico.

Start in Santa Fe. Founded by Don Pedro de Peralta 10 years before the Mayflower pilgrims arrived at Plymouth, the city is a blend of Spanish, Mexican, Native American, and European cultures. To get to the historic Santa Fe Plaza

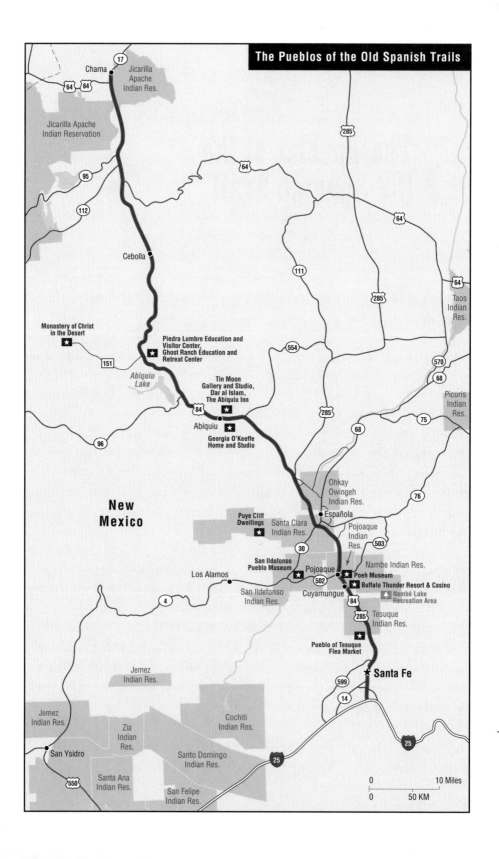

The Pueblos of the Old Spanish Trails

Santa Fe's unique architecture

from I-25, take Exit 282B, St. Francis Drive/US 84. Turn right at Cerrillos Road and continue until it merges with Galisteo Street, which dead-ends at West San Francisco Street, the plaza's southern border. Since parking can be a challenge, especially during festivals and other events, you may want to visit www.santafenm.gov for parking information and maps before you arrive.

Designated a National Historic Landmark in 1960, the 400-year-old plaza consists of a tree-lined park, bordered by a collection of restaurants, shops, and museums. For historical perspective, begin at the New Mexico History Museum, where you'll find exhibits on the state's indigenous people and Spanish Colonial, Mexican, territorial, and statehood eras. The oldest public building in the United States, the Palace of the Governors, is part of the history museum's campus.

Continue exploring Santa Fe by visiting one of its many art museums. On the plaza, check out the Museum of Contemporary Native Arts, a collection of more than 7,500 contemporary Native American works dating from 1962 to the present, or stop by the nearby New Mexico Museum of Art. Since this drive continues through O'Keeffe Country, don't miss the Georgia O'Keeffe Museum. Within walking distance of the plaza, this museum displays the famed Ameri-

The Museum of Contemporary Native Arts showcases Native American talent.

A statue of St. Francis of Assisi stands before the Santa Fe catheral that bears his name.

can Modernist's paintings and includes exhibits on her life. If you have extra time and are willing to venture away from the plaza, the Museum of Spanish Colonial Art, the Museum of Indian Arts & Culture, and Museum of International Folk Art are all located about 2 miles away on Camino Lejo.

In between museums, browse the Southwestern shops and art galleries located on the plaza. Or catch a bite to eat. Santa Fe is known for outstanding New Mexican cuisine. For breakfast or brunch, walk west along San Francisco Street to local favorite Tia Sophia's and order the eggs smothered in green chile. Later in the day, try Café Pasqual's. The dishes here are influenced by Asian and Mediterranean as well as New Mexican flavors, making it a great option for those who are unsure about the traditional, red and green chile–based entrées.

Dolls for sale in Santa Fe Plaza

Before leaving the plaza, make your way to the Loretto Chapel. Completed in 1878, the small chapel was designed with a flaw: there was no access to the choir loft 22 feet above. Carpenters concluded that a staircase would interfere with the limited interior space and recommended the chapel's sisters use a ladder. Undeterred, the sisters prayed to St. Joseph, the patron saint of carpenters, and on the ninth day, an unknown carpenter appeared asking for work. Over the next three years, he constructed a staircase with two 360-degree turns and no apparent means of support, and then he left. To this day, his identity remains a mystery.

Returning to US 84, head north with the Sangre de Cristo Mountains to your right. Just outside of Santa Fe, you'll enter the Tesuque (*Teh-sue-key*) Pueblo lands. One of the smallest pueblos with a population of just 800, it opens to the public in January for Three King's Day festivities; the first Saturday of June for the

Blessing of the Fields and Corn Dance; November 12 for San Diego Feast Day and Harvest Dances; and on Christmas Day. To visit pueblo on a feast day, watch for signs on US 84. At other times of the year, pick up a souvenir at the **Pueblo of Tesuque Flea Market**, directly off the highway at Exit 171. In addition to Puebloan crafts like baskets, carvings and pottery, you'll find clothing, antiques, fruits and vegetables, and other food.

From here, Camel Rock Casino will quickly appear on the right. Operated by the Tesuque tribe, it is the first in a series of casinos along the route. The second and most impressive of these, the **Buffalo Thunder Resort & Casino**, emerges at Exit 177, after Cuyamungue. In addition to its casino, the Hilton property includes a spa, RV park, and the Towa Golf Club. Since you're only 15 minutes from Santa Fe at this point, its location is ideal for exploring the Old Spanish Trail.

The Pueblo of Pojoaque (*Po-wock-ee* or *Po-hock-ee*) inspired the design of Buffalo Thunder Resort. You can visit the actual pueblo on January 12 for Reyes

Plan to spend several hours browsing the shops in Santa Fe.

RED OR GREEN?

When you order New Mexican cuisine, be prepared to answer, "Red or green?" New Mexicans have strong opinions when it comes to the sauce that drenches the food on their plates, with some adamantly declaring red the best and others equally passionate about green. Before you choose, you should know a thing or two about what's going on your plate.

Chiles play an integral role in New Mexican cuisine.

All chiles start off green, turning red or yellow as they mature. Green sauce consists of roasted green chiles while red sauce consists of dried red chiles that have been reconstituted and blended. Typically, the green sauce is hotter, but always ask—sometimes, depending on the chiles used in that day's batch, the red can actually pack more punch.

Can't decide? Order your dish *Christmas style,* which will give you a little of each.

Day dances and on December 12 for its Feast Day celebrations, honoring Our Lady of Guadalupe. At other times, learn more about the Pojoaque people at the Poeh Museum. From US 84, turn right at West Gutierrez Street and make an immediate right onto Cities of Gold Road. The museum will be on the left. Although run by the Pojoaque Pueblo, the museum displays exhibits devoted to all Tewa-speaking people.

Pojoaque tribe members also operate the Sports Bar Race Book and Casino, located immediately north of the museum on Cities of Gold Road, and the Cities of Gold Casino, a half mile beyond that. Both venues can be seen on the right from US 84.

At this point, you have the option of detouring to the San Ildefonso (*Ill-day-*

fon-so) Pueblo, known for its exceptional black-on-black pottery. Take the NM 502 exit, turn left toward Los Alamos for approximately 6 miles. You can visit the pueblo on January 23 for Feast Day, when tribe members perform the Buffalo, Comanche, and Deer Dances; in July for the arts & crafts fair; September 8 for the Nativity of the Blessed Virgin Mary Feast Day and for the Corn Dance; and on Christmas Day for the Matachina Dance. The **San Ildefonso Pueblo Museum** displays San Ildefonso artifacts, pottery, and other crafts.

Or you can continue half a mile along US 84 to Cundiyo Road/NM 503 and turn right to visit the Nambé (*Nam-bay*) Pueblo. After about 3 miles on Cundiyo Road, turn right again onto Nambé Pueblo 101 and drive another 4 miles to the pueblo, which is open to the public on January 6 for Buffalo, Deer, and Antelope dances; Easter for the Bow and Arrow Dance; July 4 for various dances; and Christmas Eve for the Buffalo, Deer, and Antelope dances.

But **Nambé Lake Recreation Area**, located farther along Nambé Pueblo 101, is what really makes the detour worthwhile. Fed by the Rio Nambé, the 56-acre lake in the shadow of the Sangre de Cristo Mountains is a popular destination for trout fishing. Plan to bring a picnic lunch, wade in the river, and hike the 15-minute, shaded cottonwood trail leading to the base of **Nambé Falls**. If the scenery seems familiar, it should—the rock formations here served as a backdrop for scenes from John Carpenter's *Vampires* and *City Slickers,* starring Billy Crystal.

Returning to US 84, you pass through El Valle De Arroyo Seco and enter **Española**. Although Santa Fe is the oldest existing capital in the United States, Española was the first. Don Juan de Oñate established New Mexico's first colony, San Gabriel, in Española Valley in 1598, and it remained the regional capital until Peralta, the third governor, arrived 11 years later and moved it to Santa Fe.

Despite its proud history, expect to see abandoned buildings, trash, and graffiti as you drive through Española, especially as you follow US 84 left across the Rio Grande. If you want to explore the city, follow the signs directing you to keep right for Riverside Drive/NM 68 and take a right again at Santa Cruz Road/NM 76, continuing to Plaza de Española. From the plaza, you can easily walk to Mission Museum y Convento, a replica of the original San Gabriel mission; the Bond House Museum; Veteran's Wall; and the Plaza Fountain.

The Ohkay Owingeh (*O-keh O-weeng-eh*) Pueblo, formerly the San Juan Pueblo, is also a few miles away. Four miles from where NM 68 splits from US 84, turn left on NM 74. The pueblo, 1 mile down the road, invites the public to per-

VISITING TAOS PUEBLO

Taos is a short detour from Sante Fe and can be accessed at several points along the drive. A multistoried adobe building, it has been continuously inhabited for more than 1,000 years, with approximately 150 people living in it full-time today. You can visit the pueblo Monday through Saturday, 8–4, Sunday, 8:30–4. If you plan to go in late winter to early spring, call 575-758-1028 first, since the pueblo closes each year for approximately 10 weeks. A fee is charged: $10/adults, and $5/students. Children 10 and under are free.

Each July, Taos Pueblo holds a Pow Wow, featuring dance competitions and arts and crafts. *New Mexico Tourism Department and Mike Stauffer*

The same rules apply here as they do at any pueblo. You can only photo the pueblo if you purchase a $6 permit for your camera, and you must ask tribe members' permission before photographing them. You are also asked to respect the privacy of local residents. Visit www.taos.org for a complete listing. The Web site also has a complete listing of events and traditional dances.

Ohkay Owingeh Basket Dance *Seth Roffman*

formances of the Deer Dance in late February; the Spanish drama *Los Matacines* and Pine Torch Processions on Christmas Day; and various dances throughout the year. At other times, you can experience tribal hospitality at the Ohkay Hotel and Casino, located on NM 68.

Visit the Santa Clara Pueblo by staying in the left lane on US 84, turning at Paseo de Oñate/US 84 and crossing the Rio Grande. Instead of following Paseo de Oñate north, go south on NM 30 for approximately 1 mile. The pueblo welcomes visitors on San Antonio Feast Day in June for the Comanche Dance; on Santa Clara Pueblo's Feast Day in August, when the Buffalo, Harvest, and Corn dances are performed; and year-round to tour the **Puye Cliff Dwellings**. Tickets for the Puebloan ruins tour can be purchased at the Puye Cliffs Welcome Center in the Valero Gas Station on the corner of NM 30 and Puye Cliffs Road. You will be directed from there to a bed & breakfast built by Fred Harvey in the early 1900s. Located at the base of the ruins, it serves as an interpretive center and gift shop.

To make your way through the city without stopping, however, continue on Paseo de Oñate/US 84, which curves and heads north just past the Española Valley Fiber Arts Center. The drive becomes more relaxing as you leave Española and pass through a series of small communities: El Guacho, San Jose, Hernandez, and El Duende. Watch for US 285 to split from US 84 as you approach Chili; you'll want to stay on US 84, which takes you through the Santa Fe National Forest on your way to Abiquiu.

A few miles before Abiquiu, keep your eyes open for Santa Rosa de Lima on the right side of the road. The ruins of this chapel date from the early 1700s and mark the original Spanish settlement in the area. Pets and photographs are not permitted.

The Abiquiu Inn at Milemarker 211.5 is the first clear sign that you're entering O'Keeffe Country. Situated on the banks of the Rio Chama, the casita-style inn inspires artists, writers, nature lovers, and the world-weary. After a night or two here, you'll understand why O'Keeffe left New York in 1949 to make Abiquiu her permanent home until 1986, when illness forced her to move to Santa Fe.

O'Keeffe's relationship with Northern New Mexico began in 1929. Five years after marrying Alfred Stieglitz, she spent her first summer painting the striking local rock formations and vast skies. Over the next decade, she returned several times, eventually purchasing her Ghost Ranch home in 1940. A few years later, she purchased a second home, a 5,000-sqaure-foot Spanish Colonial–era compound located in Abiquiu. Both homes are now owned by the Georgia O'Keeffe Museum, but you can only tour the second, the Georgia O'Keeffe Home and Studio. Call the museum or order tickets online.

Abiquiu has a colorful history dating back to the 1730s when the Spanish settled the area on the ruins of a prehistoric Tewa pueblo. Raiding Utes, Comanches, and other tribes forced the Spanish at times to completely abandon their community. Hoping to stabilize the region, Governor Tomás Vélez Capuchín awarded a grant permitting 34 genízaro families—detribalized Indians sold or traded to Spanish as children who were raised as Spanish-speaking Christians—to occupy the community. Today, although Abiquiu is not one of the recognized Northern pueblos, it is often referred to as the Abiquiu Pueblo, and as in any puebloan community, photographs are prohibited.

The red rocks and rugged terrain surrounding Ghost Ranch inspired artist Georgia O'Keefe. *New Mexico Tourism Department and James Orr*

For travelers using the Old Spanish Trail, Abiquiu offered the last opportunity to purchase supplies for the journey ahead, which veered northwest outside of town. As you leave, you'll be greeted by chiseled rock formations to the right. Some of the more famous are difficult to pinpoint or cannot be spotted from the road, but you can pick up a map from **Tin Moon Gallery and Studio** in Abiquiu to help locate them. The first and most impressive rock formation is El Pedernal, a huge boulder balancing on a rock spire about a mile north of Abiquiu. You also won't want to miss Plaza Blanca, which can be easily accessed from **Dar al Islam**, the mosque that owns the property. With its huge limestone and white sandstone pillars, Plaza Blanca resembles a Grecian temple.

On your left, **Abiquiu Lake Recreation Area**—a 5,200-acre reservoir available for fishing, boating, hiking, and camping—makes an impressive landscape. Turn at NM 96 to access.

Approximately 14 miles north of Abiquiu, watch for the turnoff for the **Ghost Ranch Education and Retreat Center**. The 21,000-acre ranch located in the shadow of El Monte Rojo was originally part of the Piedra Lumbre, or shining rock, land grant given to Pedro Martin Serrano in 1766 by the king of Spain. Subsequent owners Arthur and Phoebe Pack donated the property in 1955 to the Presbyterian Church, which has since used it as a conference center and retreat. You are welcome to explore the **Ruth Hall Museum of Paleontology**—the ranch is one of the richest quarries of the Triassic era and where the dinosaur Coelophysis was discovered in 1947—and the **Florence Hawley Ellis Museum of Anthropology**. If you want to spend some time renewing your spirit here, book a room, and schedule a spa treatment. Or enjoy the outdoors by hiking, kayaking at Abiquiu Lake, horseback riding, and challenging yourself on the center's rope courses.

> ## POSHUOUINGE RUINS
>
> **T**he Chama River Valley has at least a dozen major ruins and hundreds of smaller ones, including Poshuouinge (*Poe-shoo-wing-ay*) Ruins, located 2.5 miles east of Abiquiu. Watch for the parking area on the left side of US 84.

Between Milemarkers 225 and 226, you'll see the entrance for the **Piedra Lumbre Education and Visitor Center**, formerly the Ghost Ranch Living Museum. A partnership between Ghost Ranch and the Carson National Forest, the center displays exhibits on the geology, paleontology, and archaeology of the region. Other highlights include an art gallery, the Pack House, the O'Keeffe Tower, and the 1.25-acre Beaver National Forest, the nation's smallest national forest.

Forest Service Road 151 appears about a mile past the Piedra Lumbre Visitor Center. Turn left here to visit the **Monastery of Christ in the Desert**. Although it may take up to an hour to drive the unmaintained 13 miles to the monastery, it's worth the detour. The Benedictine monastery welcomes visitors to attend services at the church, shop in its gift store, mediate in the garden, stay overnight in the guesthouse (reserve online beforehand), and tour the Abbey Beverage Company, where they brew Monks' Ale and Monks' Wit.

You can easily see Echo Amphitheater, located a mile north of the monastery turnoff, from the road, but to experience its echo, follow the signs to the parking lot and take the 10-minute trek to the naturally formed sandstone theater.

As you begin to climb out of the lower Chama Valley, you leave the red rocks behind and settle in for the remaining 40 miles. The drive becomes progressively greener from here with desert shrub giving way to pines outside of Cebolla. North of this small town, cattle graze, sometimes congregating under advertisements like 1000 ACRES FOR SALE PLUS EIGHT BULL ELK PERMITS. Continue through the communities of Tierra Amarilla, Los Ojos, and Brazos, and finish in Chama, where you'll find restaurants, lodging, and the Cumbres & Toltec Scenic Railroad.

IN THE AREA

ACCOMMODATIONS

The Abiquiu Inn, 21120 US 84, Abiquiu. Call 505-685-4378. Rates begin at $80/night for an economy room and range upward to $200/night for a two-bedroom casita. Web site: www.abiquiuinn.com.

Buffalo Thunder Resort, 30 Buffalo Thunder Trail, Santa Fe. Call 877-455-7775. A Hilton resort inspired by the Pojoaque Pueblo, Buffalo Thunder offers 395 luxurious rooms, a spa, casino, and the Towa Golf Club. From $150/night. Web site: www.buffalo thunderresort.com.

Chama River Bend Lodge, 2625 US 64, Chama. Call 1-800-288-1371. Rooms from $69/night, cabins from $99/night. Web site: www.chamariver bendlodge.com.

Ghost Ranch Education and Retreat Center, Abiquiu. Call 505-685-4333. Stay in the setting that inspired O'Keeffe. Rooms with private or communal bathrooms are available, plus adobe-style units, a hacienda, tent camping, and RV spaces. Check online for rates and availability. Web site: www.ghostranch.org.

Inn of the Governors, 101 W. Alameda, Santa Fe. Call 505-982-4333 or 1-800-234-4534. Within walking distance of the plaza, this inn offers free parking, free wireless internet, and complimentary afternoon tea and sherry. Rooms from $130/night. Web site: www.innofthegovernors .com.

La Fonda on the Plaza, 100 E. San Francisco Street, Santa Fe. Call 505-982-5511 or 1-800-523-5002. This charming, historic hotel has 172 classically appointed rooms plus 14 secluded rooms in The Terrace at La Fonda. Rooms from $100/night, depending on the season. Web site: www.lafondasantafe.com.

ATTRACTIONS AND RECREATION

Abiquiu Lake Recreation Area, NM 96, Abiquiu. Managed by the United

States Army Corps of Engineers, this lake has some of the best fishing in northern New Mexico. Web site: www .spa.usace.army.mil/recreation/ab /index.htm.

Cumbres & Toltec Scenic Railroad, Chama. Call 1-888-286-2737. Originally constructed in 1880, this steam engine route takes passengers to Antonito, Colorado, beginning in May and running through mid-October. Tickets begin at $75/adults and $40/children 2–12. Web site: www .cumbrestoltec.com.

Dar al Islam, County Road 155, Abiquiu. Call 505-685-4515, ext. 21, before visiting. You wouldn't expect to find a mosque in this small desert community, but there it is. Make the visit to see the Plaza Blanca rock formations, a favorite subject of O'Keeffe's paintings. Web site: www.daral islam.org.

Georgia O'Keeffe Home and Studio, Abiquiu. Call 505-685-4539. Phone for reservations or purchase tickets online. Tours are limited to 12 people, last approximately an hour, and leave from the Abiquiu Inn. Tickets: $35– 55/person. You will not be allowed to bring purses or take photographs. Web site: www.okeeffemuseum.org /her-houses.html.

Georgia O'Keeffe Museum, 217 Johnson Street, Santa Fe. Call 505-946- 1000. A collection of more than 3,000 works including 1,149 O'Keeffe paintings, drawings and sculptures.

Open daily 10–5. Admission is $10/adults, free for children under 18. Web site: www.okeeffemuseum.org.

Ghost Ranch Education and Retreat Center, Abiquiu. Call 505-685-4333. This retreat center is also home to the Ruth Hall Museum of Paleontology and the Florence Hawley Ellis Museum of Anthropology. You can take a tour dedicated to O'Keeffe or arrange for accommodations. See Web site for tour and museum information. Web site: www.ghostranch .org.

Loretto Chapel, 207 Old Santa Fe Trail, Santa Fe. Call 505-982-0092. The staircase in this Gothic-Revival style chapel features a staircase with two 360-degree turns and no apparent means of support. Open daily; hours vary with the season. Web site: www.lorettochapel.com.

Monastery of Christ in the Desert, County Road 151, Abiquiu. Call 801- 545-8567. This Benedictine monastery has a mediation garden, gift shop and brewery, but the 13- mile drive is so treacherous it could take up to an hour to get there. Web site: www.christdesert.org.

Museum of Contemporary Native Arts, 108 Cathedral Place, Santa Fe. Call 505-983-1777. The museum showcases contemporary Native American arts dating from 1962 to the present. Open Monday and Wednesday through Saturday, 10–5, and Sunday, 12–5. Closed Tuesday.

Watch for free-roaming, domesticated animals while driving through Navajo lands.

Admission is $10/adults; half-price for seniors, students, and New Mexico residents. Web site: www.iaia.edu /museum.

Nambé Falls and Nambé Lake Recreation Area. Call 505-455-4444. Fish, picnic, and hike to a spectacular waterfall. Day use fee required. Web site: www.nambefalls.com.

New Mexico History Museum, 113 Lincoln Avenue, Santa Fe. Call 505-476-5200. Located next door to the Palace of the Governors, the history museum includes exhibits on the area's native people, Spanish colonization, the Mexican era, and the Santa Fe Trail. Open daily 10–5, with extended hours until 8 on Friday. Admission is $9/out-of-state visitors, $6/New Mexico residents, and free for children under 17. Web site: www.nmhistorymuseum.org.

Palace of the Governors, 105 W. Palace Avenue, Santa Fe. Call 505-476-5100. The oldest public building in the United States is now part of the New Mexico History Museum campus. Web site: www.palaceofthe governors.org.

Piedra Lumbre Education & Visitor Center, Abiquiu. Call 505-685-4333. The visitor center houses exhibits on geology, paleontology, archaeology, and regional history. Generally open Wednesday through Sunday, 9–5. Closed during the winter. Web site: www.ghostranch.org.

Poeh Museum, 78 Cities of Gold Road, Santa Fe. Call 505-455-5041. Exhibits include all Tewa-speaking people, not just those from the Pojoaque Pueblo, where the museum is located. Web site: www.poehmuseum .com.

Pueblo of Tesuque Flea Market, 15 Flea Market Road, Santa Fe. Purchase beads, baskets, pottery, paintings, fruits and vegetables, antiques, and more at this open-air market. Web site: www.pueblooftesuqueflea market.com.

Puye Cliff Dwellings, Santa Clara Canyon Road. Tour Puebloan ruins and the Harvey House. Tickets are available at the Valero Gas Station on the corner of NM 30 and Puye Cliffs Road, beginning at $20/adults. Web site: www.puyecliffs.com.

San Ildefonso Pueblo Museum, San Ildefonso Pueblo. Call 505-455-2273. The museum is open Monday through Friday, 8–4:30. Admission is $3/vehicle.

Tin Moon Studio and Gallery, US 84, Abiquiu. Call 505-685-4829. The gallery houses an impressive collection of artwork and provides information on local sights. Web site: www .abiquiustudiotour.org/biz/tinmoon _gallery.html.

DINING

Café Pasqual's, 121 Don Gaspar Avenue, Santa Fe. Call 505-983-9340. Named after the patron saint of kitchens and cooks, San Pasqual, this restaurant serves dishes inspired by Mexican, Mediterranean, and Asian cooking traditions. Web site: www .pasquals.com.

Galisteo Bistro & Wine Bar, 227 Galisteo Street, Santa Fe. Call 505-982-3700. If you're looking for something other than Mexican fare, Galisteo's may be the ticket. The restaurant serves international cuisine and wines from New Mexico and beyond. Web site: www.galisteobistro.com.

The High Country Restaurant and Saloon, intersection of US 84/64 and NM 17, Chama. Call 575-756-2384. This family restaurant serves hand-cut steaks, burgers, pasta, and New

New Mexico cuisine *New Mexico Tourism Department and Dan Monaghan*

Mexican cuisine. Web site: www.the highcountrychama.com.

Maria's New Mexican Kitchen, 555 W. Cordova Road, Santa Fe. Call 505-983-7929. Considered by many to be the best example of New Mexican cuisine in Santa Fe, Maria's also serves margaritas made only from 100-percent *real* tequila, triple sec, and lemon or lime juice. Web site: www.marias-santafe.com.

Tecolote Café, 1203 Cerrillos Road, Santa Fe. Call 505-988-1362. Famous for its breakfasts—try the jalapeño bacon—this restaurant was featured on Food Network's *Diners, Drive-Ins and Dives*. Web site: www.tecolote cafe.com.

Tia Sophia's, 210 W. San Francisco Street, Santa Fe. Call 505-983-9880. A local favorite serving breakfast, lunch, and dinner.

OTHER CONTACTS

Abiquiu & Around. The Web site has a visitor map, lodging and food options, and local attraction listings. Web site: www.abiquiuandaround .org.

City of Española, 405 N. Paseo de Oñate, Española. Call 505-747-6100. Click on the visitors' tab at the city's Web site for local tourist information and a map. Web site: www.cityof espanola.org.

Old Spanish Trail. Call 505-988-6098. Web site: www.nps.gov/olsp.

Old Spanish Trail Association. Call 505-425-6039. The Web site provides resources for exploring the Spanish Trail and learning more about its history. Web site: www.oldspanishtrail .org.

Santa Fe Convention & Visitors Bureau, 201 W. Marcy Street, Santa Fe. Call 505-955-6200 or 1-800-777-2489. Web site: www.santafe.org.

Stairs leading up to the top of El Morro where you'll find the ruins of Atsinna

6 The Artists of the Zuni Mountains

Estimated length: 75 miles to the Zuni Pueblo

Estimated time: 1.5 hours to the Zuni Pueblo

Getting there: From Albuquerque, take I-40 to Exit 85. Drive through Grants to NM 53. Or bypass Grants, taking I-40 directly to Exit 81 for NM 53. You can also complete this drive in reverse. From Flagstaff, take I-40 to Exit 339 for US 191. Go south approximately 20 miles to AZ 61. Six miles later, you cross the Arizona–New Mexico border. Continue to the Zuni Pueblo.

Highlights: Shop for arts and crafts on the Ancient Way Arts Trail, visit a wolf sanctuary, and explore Zuni culture at New Mexico's largest pueblo community. There are also two national monuments along the way, El Morro and El Malpais; a wolf sanctuary; an ice cave; and a volcanic cinder cone.

No one is really sure how long people have lived in the region, but between 1300 and 1500 A.D., the ancestors of the present-day tribe founded Zuni Pueblo and other, smaller villages. Over time, the tribe consolidated, and today, most of its 12,000 members live at the pueblo, the largest of New Mexico's 19 pueblos, and its suburb, Black Rock.

With almost 80 percent of Zuni families somehow involved in the arts, it seems natural that NM 53, which cuts through the reservation, has been designated the Ancient Way Arts Trail. Twenty-seven galleries and artistic stops from Grants to the pueblo, including nearby Gallup, feature the work of more than 650 local artists. Visit the trail's Web site (www.ancientwayartstrail.com) for details on all 27 sites.

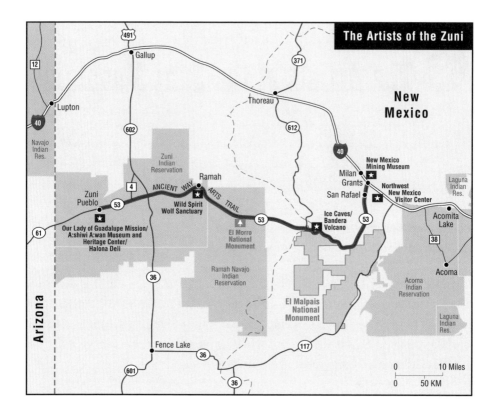

The drive actually begins before NM 53 and the arts trail. Take Exit 85 and head south of I-40 to the **Northwest New Mexico Visitor Center** for an overview of the upcoming destinations. The center has hiking guides and resources for planning up to nine suggested area tours. You can also watch more than 50 titles, including the award-winning film, *Remembered Earth,* in the 60-seat theater.

After leaving the visitor center, take NM 117 back across I-40, where the road becomes East Santa Fe Avenue in downtown Grants. Formerly a station for the Santa Fe Railroad, the town was first called Grants Camp, then Grants Station, and finally just Grants after the Grants brothers, three Canadian brothers who worked as contractors for the railroad. The town initially prospered by logging the pine trees of the nearby Zuni Mountains and then gained a reputation as the carrot capital of the United States. In 1950, a Navajo shepherd, Paddy Martinez, discovered uranium in the area sparking a 30-year mining boom.

You can learn about the history of Grants at the **New Mexico Mining Museum**, which exhibits displays on railroading, logging, ranching, and uranium mining. The museum also has a recreated uranium mine, Section 26. Descend into the mineshaft for a self-guided tour that takes you past the uranium loading and unloading station to learn about drilling, blasting, and the tight, dusty confines underground. If you have claustrophobia, you may want to restrict yourself to the above-ground experience.

Follow East Santa Fe Avenue through Grants, stopping for a meal or to shop at one of the arts-trail galleries, if you have time. At the west end of town, you'll

ANCIENT WAY ARTS TRAIL

The Ancient Way Arts Trail features 27 sites representing more than 650 local artists. A detailed map can be found online at www.ancientwayartstrail.com, but here are a few of the highlights:

❖ **Double 6 Gallery,** 1001 W. Santa Fe Avenue, Grants. Call 505-287-7311.

❖ **Inscription Rock Trading & Coffee Co.,** 1 mile east of El Morro National Monument, NM 53. Call 505-783-4706. While shopping for Native American arts and crafts, you can sip coffee, smoothies, and teas, and munch on gourmet snacks. Web site: www.inscriptionrock trading.com.

❖ **Old School Gallery,** 1.5 miles east of El Morro, NM 53. Call 505-783-4710. The gallery is open Thursday through Monday, 11–5. Web site: www.elmorro-arts.org.

❖ **Oso Ridge Spinning & Weaving School,** 7827 Zuni Canyon Road, Grants. Call 505-783-4303.

❖ **Ramah Navajo Weavers Association,** Indian Route 125, Pine Hill. Call 505-775-3254. Learn traditional Navajo methods of wool preparation, hand spinning, and weaving. Then, shop for rugs, pillows, and more.

❖ **Silver Rain Jewelry,** 1449B NM 53, Zuni. Call 505-782-2490.

❖ **Tierra Madre Arts Gallery,** 689 Oso Ridge Road, Grants. Call 800-856-5776. Located in the Cimarron Rose Bed & Breakfast.

❖ **Zuni Visitor & Arts Center,** 1239 NM 53, Zuni. Call 505-782-7238.

ACOMA

Sky City, as the Acoma Pueblo is often called, sits perched atop a 70-acre sandstone mesa that rises 367 feet above the valley floor, and like Old Orabai on the Hopi Reservation in Arizona, it claims to be the oldest continuously inhabited community in the United States. Fewer than 50 Acomans still live on the top of the mesa today, but you can tour the pueblo for a fee of $20/adults, $17/seniors, and $12/children. A family rate of $55 for two adults and two children is also available.

Acoma pottery for sale

Purchase your tickets at the Sky City Cultural Center. From there, you'll take a bus to the mesa top where tours begin in the San Esteban del Rey Mission. As your guide loops through the village, you are encouraged to visit with local artists and purchase Zuni crafts. If you purchased a camera permit ($10), feel free to take photos of more than 250 dwellings, outdoor ovens, and open views.

Back at the cultural center, visit the Haak'u Museum, which showcases Zuni artwork, and enjoy lunch at the Y'aak'a Café. The center is open daily 9–5. Tours begin at 9:30 through 3:30. Check online at www.acomaskycity.org for more information and for a calendar of feast days and pueblo closures.

want to turn left at NM 53 and drive south through San Rafael. The trail-heads of **El Malpais National Monument and National Conservation Area** appear soon after leaving the largely Hispanic farming community. Watch for the Zuni Acoma Trail, an ancient path that once connected the Pueblo of Zuni with the Pueblo of Acoma, at Milemarker 70, followed by the El Calderon Trail at Milemarker 66. Two miles down the road, the El Malpais Information Center will be on your left. Check in here for scenic driving and hiking information.

El Malpais means "badlands" in Spanish, a moniker early explorers gave to any volcanic area. It was formed approximately 10,000 years ago when magma erupted from what is today Bandera Crater. For the next several years, fluid lava flowed from its base, creating a series of lava rivers. As the outer lava cooled and hardened, the hot lava continued to flow under-

The lava fields near Bandera Volcano

neath. The result was a 17-mile mile lava tube system, the longest in the continental United States. While most of the tube system has collapsed, several sections remain intact as cave structures.

Until recently, you could enter the caves, but these have been closed indefinitely to protect local bats from disease. Rangers plan to allow limited access by permit in the future; however, in the meantime, you will have to limit yourself to hiking in and driving through El Malpais. Note that the national monument covers 350,000 acres, and not all of the hikes or overlooks can be accessed by NM 53. Some, like Sandstone Bluffs Overlook and the Garrett Homestead, branch off NM 117.

It's less than 3 miles from the El Malpais Information Center to the Ice Caves and Bandera Volcano. Turn left off NM 53 at Milemarker 61 and follow the dirt road to the small trading post that also serves as a visitor center. In the 1930s, this building was a saloon and dancehall, and ice mined from the Ice Cave kept the establishment's beer cold. Now it displays Native American artifacts found on the family-owned and operated property as well as sells contemporary artwork. Purchase your tickets here.

Tackle the Bandera Volcano first by picking up the trail behind the trading post. You won't have any trouble with the first section of the trail since it is relatively level. As you begin to climb the side of the volcano, the trail gradually inclines 5 to 10 percent. You can see the cinder cone without climbing to the top, but if you decide to continue, the last third of the trail levels out and isn't too difficult. Make sure to bring plenty of water.

After you finish exploring the Bandera Volcano, return to the visitor center and take the trail south of the building. The level walk curves through a lava field

It's a constant 31 degrees in the Ice Cave.

El Morro was an oasis for weary travelers.

toward the cave. Using the handout you received at the visitor center, you should be able to locate the Ancestral Puebloan ruins at Stop 6. Humans have lived in the area for centuries, adapting the caves into temporary shelters and even refrigerators.

For the last portion of the trail, you will have to walk down 69 steps to see the 20-foot thick, algae-tinted ice at the bottom of the cave. As rain collects and snow melts, the water seeps into the cave and freezes, and since the temperature remains a constant 31 degrees, it never melts. Unfortunately, you'll have to climb back up those same 69 steps. Don't worry—the wooden staircase is divided into three sections, each with a rest area and bench.

Returning to NM 53, you drive through a 16-mile stretch of cattle and Ponderosa Pines. Look to the right. The Zuni Mountains run from roughly I-40 south to NM 53 and from Gallup east to Grants; they sit on the Continental Divide,

The trail to Inscription Rock is an easy, paved loop.

which you'll pass near Milemarker 51. Less than 10 miles from this point, you'll see the sign for El Morro National Monument. Turn left and enter the monument.

As you drive to the visitor center, you'll pass two pullouts where you can take a panoramic photograph of the large sandstone rock rising 200 feet above the valley floor. Spanish explorers called it *El Morro,* or The Headland, and rested near the natural pool at its base. While there, they added to the Ancestral Puebloan petroglyphs by carving names and dates into the soft rock of El Morro's walls. More than 2,000 signatures, dates, messages, and petroglyphs cover the area.

You'll need to stop at the visitor center to pay admission and pick up the guide to the inscriptions. There are two hikes to consider. The first is a paved, half-mile loop that takes you past the pool and the carvings on Inscription Rock. Highlights include an inscription by Governor Don Juan de Onate in 1605, 15 years before pilgrims landed at Plymouth Rock; P. Gilmer Breckinridge of Virginia, part of Lieutenant Edward F. Beale's engineer corps; and the first English inscription, which misspelled the word *inscription* as *insciption,* without the *r.*

Inscriptions carved by travelers at El Morro National Monument

The second hike branches off the Inscription Rock Trail at the end of the inscription wall and climbs up to the mesa's top, where you'll find Atsinna Pueblo, a multistory structure of at least 875 rooms that was believed to have housed up to 1,500 people. Before you set out on the Mesa Top Trail, ask the rangers about the weather. You don't want to be on top during a lighting storm. In all, expect to spend about an hour at the monument if you want to stick to the shorter hike and two hours to complete the longer one.

From El Morro National Monument, it's approximately 10 miles to Ramah, a Mormon farming community established in 1876 next to the isolated, 25-mile-long by 15-mile-wide Ramah Navajo Reservation. As you enter the community,

THE RAMAH NAVAJO RESERVATION

This isolated section of the Navajo Reservation, which acts independently of the rest of the Navajo nation, has occupied the land around Ramah since 1540 when they came to the aid of the Zunis against Francisco Vásquez de Coronado. Their reservation is just 25 miles long and 15 miles wide.

watch on your left for the Wild Spirit Wolf Sanctuary. Home to more than 50 wolves and wolf-dogs, the sanctuary offers tours four times a day. You'll learn about the sanctuary, wolves in the wild, and why wolves don't make good pets. Enhance your experience by camping in the primitive campground across the street. If you're lucky, you'll hear the wolves howl at the moon.

Other local attractions include the Plaza Del Sol gift shop, the Lady Stagecoach Café, and Lake Ramah. There's also the tiny Ramah Museum with one room devoted to pioneer relics, another to Ancestral Puebloan artifacts, and a third to local military veterans.

After leaving Ramah, you'll cross the Rio Pescado River and the few remaining buildings of Pescado. The turnoff for Fence Lake is located at Milemarker 22.

The Zuni Pueblo welcomes visitors

VISITING GALLUP

Gallup is a half-hour side trip from NM 53 via NM 602 and one of the major stopping points along I-40.

Since the 1890s, when traders first set up outlets in Gallup, the town has been a major distribution point for Native American arts and crafts. You can visit several of these historic trading post outlets while in town, including Richardsons Trading Company (www.richardsontrading.ecrater.com), Ellis Tanner Trading Company (www.etanner.com), and Joe Milo's Trading Company (www.joemilo.com). The Gallup Cultural Center, located in the Old Trail Station, is also worth a visit. It sells Navajo, Zuni, and Hopi art to raise funds for the Southwest Indian Foundation, a nonprofit organization that helps Native Americans in need.

Native Americans perform at the Gallup Inter-Tribal Indian Ceremonial
New Mexico Tourism Department and Mike Stauffer

Every August, Gallup also hosts the Inter-Tribal Indian Ceremonial at Red Rock Park. The five-day event features ceremonial dances performed by tribes from around the world, a marketplace of Indian fine arts, a rodeo, and parade. Admission is $10/person before 4, plus $5/vehicle for parking. If you go after 4, admission is free.

Don't miss the A:Shiwi A:wan Museum at the Zuni Pueblo.

Ironically, Fence Lake isn't really a lake. It's largely ranchland with a few businesses. Legend has it the name Fence Lake comes from the original settlers having fenced off a natural pond in the area.

Entering the Zuni Pueblo, you technically don't need to stop at the visitor center—you could shop at the stores, grab a bite to eat, and tour the Zuni museum without reporting in—but you should drop by. This is where you'll learn about any dances or ceremonies at the plaza and where you can purchase tickets for tours of **Our Lady of Guadalupe Mission** and of the Middle Village, the cultural heart of the village. With advance notice, you can also schedule to tour an artist's workshop, enjoy a traditional Zuni meal of stew and oven bread, or tour the nearby archaeological sites of Hawikku and Village of the Great Kiva. Go online at www.zunitourism.com to learn more about the tours, and call 505-782-7238 to arrange for a tour requiring advance notice.

Also at the visitor center, you can purchase a camera permit for $10/camera allowing you to take photos while in town. The tribe member who sells you the permit will detail what you can and can't take photos of, but it boils down to this: you can take photos of buildings and people with their permission. Violate these rules or take photos without a permit and your camera will be confiscated. My advice is to save the money and skip the permit. Just put your camera away. There isn't much to photograph anyway, and even if you have a permit, you will not be allowed to take pictures of tribal ceremonies.

Tribe members at the visitor center will also give you a hand-drawn map to refer to while in town. Use it to find the bakery, art galleries, and **A:Shiwi A:wan Museum & Heritage Center**, a definite must while in town. Although the village is easy to navigate, finding the museum can be a tricky. Turn left at Pia Mesa Road. You'll drive less than a mile and come to a four-way stop. Because the road curves here, Halona Plaza will be directly in front of you at this intersection. To your left will be the Christian Reform Mission School; to your right, you'll see a dirt lot. Across the lot is the museum.

It doesn't look like much from the outside—it's just a stucco building with a turquoise-colored overhang and beige coverings over the windows—but inside,

Hanola Deli, inside the Hanola Plaza, serves great green chile cheeseburgers.

you loop through exhibits detailing 500 years of Zuni history, beginning with the arrival of the Spanish explorers and ending with the tribe today. Budget at least 45 minutes.

When you finish at the museum, plan on eating at the Halona Deli. Located inside the building emblazoned with HALONA PLAZA in bright pink and turquoise, the deli serves burgers and fried chicken. Enter and walk to the back of this small grocery store to place your order. (Hint: The green chile cheeseburger is listed on New Mexico's Green Chile Cheeseburger Trail.) For about $4, you'll get a large burger, a mound of fries, and a soda, which you can eat in the six-table dining room to the right.

From this point, you can backtrack on NM 53 a few miles to NM 602 and head north to Gallup. Or, continue on NM 53 to the Arizona border, where it becomes AZ 61. This highway runs into US 191, 20 miles south of I-40.

IN THE AREA

ACCOMMODATIONS

Cimarron Rose Bed & Breakfast, NM 53, Grants. Call 1-800-856-5776. Located on 20 acres of Ponderosa forest, the inn is a bird lover's paradise, with excellent hiking, mountain biking, and cross-country skiing nearby. Gourmet breakfasts served daily. Suite rates begin at $110/night for three- to five-night stays. Web site: www.cimarronrose.com.

El Morro RV Park & Cabins, NM 53, El Morro. Call 505-783-4612. The accommodations at this site near El Morro National Monument include furnished cabins, full hook-up RV sites, and tent spaces. Small cabins with a queen-sized bed and standard-sized mattress in the loft start at $79/night, while the large cabins featuring a king- or queen-sized bed and a trundle start at $94/night. RV rates are $25/day, tent sites $12/day. Web site: www.elmorro-nm.com.

The Inn at Halona Bed & Breakfast, 23B Pia Mesa Road, Zuni. Call 505-782-4547. It doesn't look like much, especially when you enter through the general store to check in, but the charming inn at the back of the property has two patios and complimentary breakfast with Zuni touches such as blue corn pancakes and freshly made salsa. Web site: www.halona.com.

ATTRACTIONS AND RECREATION

Ancient Way Arts Trail, NM 53. Twenty-seven participating sites represent more than 650 artists and showcase the Zuni, Navajo, Hispanic, and Anglo cultures. On the last weekend in May and the first weekend in

October, the trail hosts art festivals. See the Web site for more details. Free. Web site: www.ancientwayarts trail.com.

A:Shiwi A:wan Museum & Heritage Center, 02 E. Ojo Caliente Road, Zuni. Call 505-782-4403. This small museum doesn't look like much from the outside, but it is surprisingly well done. Displays share 500 years of cultural history. Don't miss the hand-painted migration story murals. Web site: www.ashiwi-museum.org.

El Malpais National Monument and National Conservation Area, I-40 Exit 81 to NM 53. Call 505-783-4774 for the information center or 505-280-2918 for the ranger station. Formed approximately 10,000 years ago, this 350,000-acre lava field contains scenic drives and hiking trails. Until recently, you could enter the lava tubes and caves, but these have been closed indefinitely to protect local bats from white-nose syndrome. At some point, however, rangers plan to allow limited access to the caves on a permit-only basis. Except for Sandstone Bluffs Overlook, which closes at dusk, the national monument is always open. The El Malpais Information Center is open daily 8:30–4:30. Free. Web site: www.nps .gov/elma.

El Morro National Monument, NM 53, El Morro. Call 505-783-4226. For centuries, the natural pool served as an oasis for weary travelers from the Ancestral Puebloans to Spanish explorers to Anglo pioneers and soldiers. To commemorate their visit, these travelers carved pictures, dates, and names on Inscription Rock. In addition to the short trail, a longer trail takes you to the top of the bluff to see Atsinna, an Ancestral Puebloan ruin. Although the visitor center opens at 9, it closes between 5 and 7, depending on the season. Admission is $3/person over the age of 16. Web site: www.nps.gov/elmo.

Ice Caves and Bandera Volcano, Milemarker 61 on NM 53. The family-owned property has a volcanic cinder cone and a cave with an ice floor. Dirt trails lead from the trading post to both locations. The site opens at 8, but closing times vary (4, 5, or 6) depending on the season. Admission is $10/adults, $9/seniors and military, and $5/children 5–12. Web site: www .icecaves.com.

New Mexico Mining Museum, 100 N. Iron Avenue, Grants. Call 1-800-748-2142. The museum houses displays on railroading, logging, and ranching, but the highlight is Section 26, the recreated uranium mine. Visitors descend a short distance into the shaft on a self-guided tour to learn about drilling, blasting, and other aspects of the mining process. Back in the museum, there are additional displays featuring gems, minerals, and Ancestral Puebloan artifacts. The museum is open Monday through Saturday, 9–

4. Admission is $3/adults and $2/ seniors and children 7–18.

Northwest New Mexico Visitor Center, Exit 85 on I-40. The visitor center features exhibits on the land and people of northwest New Mexico, a 60-seat theater with more than 50 titles to choose from, and a bookstore with topographic maps, field guides, and other resources. It also regularly hosts astronomy programs after dark.

Our Lady of Guadalupe Mission, Zuni. Call 505-782-7238. Tours are available of the 1629 Spanish Colonial mission at 10, 1, and 3. A fee of $10/person is charged, with an additional $5/person charge for a special presentation by Alex Seowtewa, who designed the mission's interior murals. Arrangements for the artist tour must be made in advance.

Pueblo of Zuni, Zuni. Call 505-782-7000. Check in at the visitor center when you arrive for a village map, visitor information, and photography permit. You can also learn about tours to Our Lady of Guadalupe Mission, the middle village, artists' workshops, and archeological sites. In the village, you can also tour the A:Shiwi A:wan Museum & Heritage Center, shop at local stores, or eat at a local restaurant, like the Halona Deli.

Wild Spirit Wolf Sanctuary, 378 Candy Kitchen Road, Ramah. Call 505-775-3304. The 80-acre sanctuary gives one-hour tours of their facility to learn about their 50-plus wolves and wolf-dogs—their behaviors and characteristics, why wolves make poor pets, and how the sanctuary cares for their animals. Special arrangements can be made for a photography tour. If you want to hear the wolves howl at the moon, camp across the street in the primitive campground for $15/night. Admission is $7/adults, $6/seniors, and $4/children. Kids under 7 are free. Tours are available Tuesday through Sunday at 11, 12:30, 2, and 3:30. Web site: www .wildspiritwolfsanctuary.org.

DINING

Ancient Way Café, NM 53, El Morro. Call 505-783-4612. Part of the El Morro RV Park & Cabins, this restaurant earns its own listing. The menu is a mix of American, New Mexican, and vegetarian entrées. During winter months, there may be only one or two items available. But don't worry. They *will* be good. Web site: www.el morro-nm.com.

Chu Chu's, NM 53, Zuni. Call 505-782-2100. Try pizza, calzones, sandwiches, or the blue corn enchiladas.

El Cafecito, 820 E. Santa Fe Avenue, Grants. Call 505-285-6229. This café delivers solid New Mexican food and Mexican favorites like tacos, enchiladas, and chimichangas. Try the stuffed sopapillas.

Halona Deli, 23B Pia Mesa Road, Zuni. Don't be intimidated by the rundown exterior or by the fact that you have to walk to the back of a grocery store to place your order. The green chile cheeseburger is so good that it's one of the stops on New Mexico's Green Chile Cheeseburger Trail. Seating is available. Web site: www.halona.com.

La Ventana Steakhouse, 110½ Geis Street, Grants. Call 505-287-9393. A white-tablecloth restaurant with a full bar, La Ventana serves steaks, pasta, New Mexican food, and more. Web site: www.thelaventana.com.

OTHER CONTACTS

Cibola National Forest and National Grasslands. Call 505-346-3900. Portions of the drive area located within the forest. Learn about recreational opportunities online. Web site: www .fs.usda.gov.

Grants Chamber of Commerce, Grants. Call 505-287-4802. The chamber Web site lists area dining and lodging options, as well as things to do. Web site: www.grants.org.

Pueblo of Zuni, Zuni. Call 505-782-7000. Information on Zuni people, government, local events, and more. Web site: www.ashiwi.org.

Zuni Pueblo Department of Tourism, Zuni. Call 505-782-7238. This online planning guide provides additional information on the pueblo's history and culture. Check out the articles on Zuni pottery and Zuni jewelry. Web site: www.zunitourism.com.

The sandstone spire known as Spider Rock rises 800 feet above the floor of Canyon de Chelly.

7 The Heart of the Navajo Nation

Estimated length: 100 miles to Canyon de Chelly
Estimated time: 3 hours to Canyon de Chelly

Getting there: From Phoenix, take I-17 north to Flagstaff. At I-40, head west to Lupton. Take Exit 357 and go north on Indian Route 12. From Albuquerque, take I-40 into Arizona. Exit in Lupton on Indian Route 12.

Highlights: The most scenic drive in the Navajo Nation, Indian Route 12 also winds through the city of Window Rock, where tribal leaders convene at the Navajo Council Chambers. You can watch when they are in session. At Window Rock, you can also visit the Navajo Nation Museum and the Navajo Nation Zoo. Recreational activities abound at Bowl Canyon Recreational Area and Wheatfield Lake. This trip ends at Canyon de Chelly, where you can hire a Navajo guide to escort you to Ancestral Puebloan ruins.

The Dine'tah Scenic Byway runs north from Lupton to Fort Defiance and west from Tsaile to Chinle and Canyon de Chelly. As you leave Lupton, also known as *Tsedijooli,* or Round Rock, you will immediately notice the red sandstone cliffs of Helena Canyon. It's from these cliffs that Lupton takes its Navajo name and from these cliffs that the Painted Cliffs Welcome Center on the Arizona–New Mexico border takes its name.

Over the years, several movies have been filmed in the Lupton area, including *Distant Drums, Ace in the Hole,* and *The Hallelujah Trails.* It's easy to imagine Hollywood wagon trains lurching down a dirt road and mounted stuntmen charging along the cliffs as you drive through the Navajo Nation Forest. Even the small

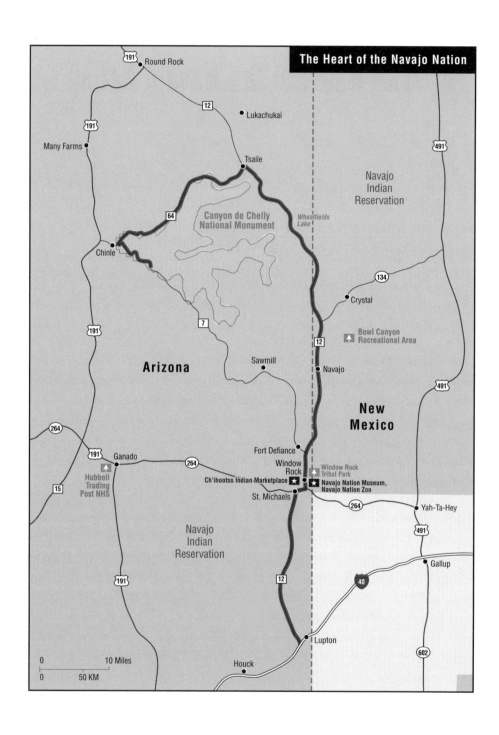

The Heart of the Navajo Nation

community of Oak Springs, with its modern conveniences, seems lost in time. You'll see horses roaming in open fields, and hogans—the traditional Navajo home—next to their present-day counterparts.

St. Michaels appears at Mile-marker 23. Known as *Ts'ihootso,* or Mountainside Meadow in Navajo, it was established with the construction of the St. Michaels Mission of Franciscan Friars in 1898. Four years later, the mission's school, the Saint Michael Indian School, opened; it still operates today. If you have time, stop by the St.

> ## SHARING THE ROAD
>
> It's not uncommon to encounter animals in the road while driving through rural areas like Indian Route 64 between Tsaile and Chinle. Watch for sheep, dogs, goats, horses, you name it, to appear on the asphalt ahead. Think you don't have to be quite as careful in town? Think again. I've seen cows in the right hand lane in Chinle.

Michaels Historical Museum. Although it is located in a subdivided stone building, it offers good insight into the Navajo culture of the early 20th century.

Getting from St. Michaels to Window Rock Tribal Park can be tricky. From the point you cross St. Michael Mission Road on the left, you'll have less than 2 miles to the intersection of Indian Route 12 and AZ 264. Turn right at the stop light. Indian Route 12 jogs along AZ 264 for 2 miles and then heads north to Fort Defiance. Later, you will turn left on to Indian Route 12 and go north, but for now, drive through on AZ 264.

Less than half a mile past this second intersection, you will see the Navajo Nation Museum, a contemporary building on the left. The free museum showcases the work of Navajo artists and includes exhibits on the Long Walk, Chief Manuelito, and the Navajo way of life. Across the parking lot, in a small basin dotted with red sandstone formations called The Haystacks, the Navajo Nation Zoological and Botanical Park houses animals common to the Navajo Reservation like elk, red foxes, and bald eagles. (The botanical park is virtually nonexistent.) Both the museum and the zoo are small, and neither takes much time to visit. Expect to spend 45 minutes at each.

As you leave the museum parking lot, turn right on AZ 264 and backtrack half a mile to the stoplight. Turn right again, this time onto Indian Route 12 toward Fort Defiance. Note the Ch'ihootso Indian Marketplace on your left. Navajo

THE LONG WALK

In 1861, as the Navajo people fought to maintain control of their traditions, General James Carlton devised a plan to remove them from their lands and send them to Bosque Redondo, a designated area along the Pecos River in New Mexico. Carlton hired Christopher "Kit" Carson to lead a force of 700 soldiers into the area, and enacting Carlton's plan, Carson ordered the torching of Navajo homes, burning of their fields, destruction of their orchards, and confiscation of their livestock. By the end of 1863, the Navajo were starving. Trusting Carson that they would be well fed by the United States Army, they surrendered.

Carson marched the Navajo at gunpoint more than 300 miles to Bosque Redondo, known today as Fort Sumner. As they marched through harsh winter conditions, nearly 200 of the 8,500 men, women, and children died of cold and starvation. Once they arrived, even more died as a result of brackish water, limited food, crop infestation, and disease. In 1868, realizing their attempt to Americanize the Navajo had failed, the U.S. government granted them sovereignty and allowed them to return to their homelands.

The Navajo Nation Museum in Window Rock and the Explore Navajo Interactive Museum in Tuba City both have exhibits on the Long Walk.

vendors sell jewelry, crafts, and other treasures here, and you can sample traditional Navajo fare at the market's indoor food stands.

The last time I drove this route, in June 2011, the sign directing you to Window Rock Tribal Park had been spray painted over, tagged to the point that it was unreadable. You should be able to find the park without the sign, though. At the first stoplight along northbound Indian Route 12, turn right. This is Tribal Hill Drive (also Indian Route 100), and it takes you into the administrative center of the Navajo Nation's tribal government. Follow it to the Navajo Nation Council Chambers, a hogan-shaped building, on the left. Eighty-eight council delegates representing 110 Navajo Nation chapters convene here four times a year in tribal meetings that are open to the public. When the council is not in session, you can tour the council chambers where Navajo artist Gerald Nailor's murals depict the Diné history and way of life.

The infamous natural arch at Window Rock Tribal Park

The Code Talkers Memorial at Window Rock Tribal Park

Just past the council chambers, the road veers right and ends at **Window Rock Tribal Park**. The park provides views of the natural sandstone arch from which the town takes its name. It is also home to a horseshoe-shaped veteran's park. Start at the Code Talkers Memorial, dedicated to the Navajo soldiers who used their native language to create a code that was never broken by our World War II enemies. Next, you'll come to a healing sanctuary featuring a sandstone fountain. As you continue, 16 angled steel pillars and memorial panels honor veterans from the Navajo Nation.

After your visit, take Tribal Hill Drive back to Indian Route 12 and turn right. Fort Defiance is less than 10 minutes to the north. Constructed as an isolated military outpost in the 1850s, the fort deteriorated during the Civil War. In 1868, it was converted to the Navajo Agency and today boasts Fort Defiance Indian Hospital. Look for the Conoco gas station on the right side as you enter town, and turn right to continue on Indian Route 12. Within a few miles, you cross over into New Mexico.

Navajo, New Mexico, sits approximately 12 miles north of Fort Defiance. The Diné people call it *Ni'iijíní,* or "place where sawing is done," because the tribe built a new state-of-the-art sawmill here in 1962. You can see the remains of the graffiti-covered sawmill, which closed in 1994, on the northern edge of town.

Take a short detour at this point to **Bowl Canyon Recreation Area**. Indian Service Route 31 is unmarked but easy to find; it runs alongside the sawmill's northern edge. You won't have to go far on this choppy but drivable dirt road to appreciate the beauty. The landscape rolls out like a verdant carpet surrounded

A short detour towards Bowl Canyon Recreation Area rewards with incredible landscapes.

by red canyon walls, a virtual oasis in the Navajo desert. If you want, you can take this road all the way to a 36-acre alpine lake, Asááyi (*Ah-sy-yeh*) Lake. Or you can head back to Indian Route 12 at any point.

As you continue north, the rocks shift from red to pale green to red again. The Navajo call the green rock formation Green Knobs, and it's the result of volcanic activity that caused peridotite, an igneous rock consisting of the minerals olivine and pyroxene, to cover the area. You won't have to look too hard to see it; it's hard to miss at Milemarker 58.

Less than 10 miles before you reach the community of Wheatfields, you cross back into Arizona. Not surprisingly, Wheatfields is named for the wheat fields Colonel John M. Washington discovered when he traveled through the area in 1849. Instead of lush fields of wheat, today you'll pass Lake Wheatfield, fed by Wheatfields Creek and runoff from the Chuska Mountains. The lake is one of the most popular fishing destinations on the Navajo Reservation, and you can purchase a tribal fishing license in Navajo, Wheatfields, or Tsaile.

Ruins in Canyon de Chelly National Monument

Mummy Cave in Canyon de Chelly National Monument

Tsaile marks the end of the drive along Indian Route 12. Named for the creek of the same name, this community is home to the main campus of Diné College, the first tribally controlled community college in the United States. The campus includes 10 residence halls, a cultural center, library, student union, college press, and the Hatathli Museum and Art Gallery. After passing the entrance to the college, turn left at Indian 64 and head toward Canyon de Chelly National Monument and Chinle.

It's about 25 miles from Tsaile to Chinle and the mouth of Canyon de Chelly, but at Milemarker 13, you can catch your first glimpse of the canyon at the Massacre Cave and Mummy Cave overlooks. Massacre Cave takes its name from a bloody incident in 1805 when Antonio de Narbona reported killing 90 warriors and 25 women and children. The Navajo, however, claim that the men were away hunting at the time and Narbona's troops killed mostly women, children, and old

HUBBELL TRADING POST

A visit to the Hubbell Trading Post, located about 40 miles south of Chinle in Ganado, takes you back nearly 135 years to a time when John Lorenzo Hubbell supplied the Navajo people with staples like flour, sugar, canned goods, and coffee in exchange for rugs, jewelry, baskets, pottery, wool, and even sheep. Hubbell purchased the post in 1878, and over the years he developed lifelong friendships with the Navajo and even made a failed run for the United States Senate. He died in 1930.

Today, you can still purchase Navajo crafts at the oldest continuously operated trading post in the country, as well as take a self-guided tour of the original Hubbell home. And if you're lucky, you might see a transaction in progress—local artists still bring their works to the post, although they're more likely to negotiate for a cash amount than flour.

Hubbell Trading Post is open 8–6 during the summer and 8–5 during the winter. Call 928-755-3475 for more information. Web site: www.nps .gov/hutr.

men huddled in an inaccessible alcove. Mummy Cave, on the other hand, has views of one of the largest Ancestral Puebloan villages in Canyon de Chelly.

There are three overlooks on the North Rim, including Antelope House, and seven on the South Rim. Plan on spending the night in Chinle to allow yourself ample time to explore the canyon the next day. The National Park Service recommends allowing four hours to visit all 10 overlooks. Add an additional two hours to hike the 2.5-mile, roundtrip trail to the White House Ruins, the only place in the park where you can go into the canyon without a Navajo guide.

Even if you have only limited time, turn left at Indian Route 7/South Rim Drive, and at least stop at the White House and Spider Rock overlooks. White House Overlook provides a clear view of ruins occupied by the Ancient Puebloan between 1060 and 1275 A.D. The ruins take their name from the white and yellow structure 30 feet above the canyon floor. Spider Rock rises 800 feet above the canyon floor. According to legend, Spider Woman, who taught the Navajo how to weave, lives at the top of this sandstone spire. Some say she comes down at night to steal away naughty children and devour them.

If you are able to spend extra time at Canyon de Chelly, hire a guide and go

You'll get a different perspective of Canyon de Chelly on a jeep tour.

White House ruins in Canyon de Chelly

into the canyon itself. You can find your guide through the local hotels or by requesting a list of guides from the visitor center. Most visitors opt to take jeep tours, but guided hikes and horseback rides are also available.

You'd be surprised at how much you miss from the rim of the 26-mile canyon. Down in the canyon, you'll see petroglyphs (images carved into the sandstone) and pictographs (images painted on the canyon walls). Ruins that you can't see from above become obvious as you look upward. According to the National Park Service, there are approximately 3,000 archaeological sites and 1,200 dwellings in the canyons that make up Canyon de Chelly.

Chinle sits west of Canyon de Chelly on Indian Route 7. From here, you can continue south to Hopiland or take Indian Route 7 west to US 191 and go south to I-40.

IN THE AREA

ACCOMMODATIONS

Best Western Canyon de Chelly Inn, 100 E. Main Street, Chinle. Call 928-674-5874. The affordable accommodations include use of the indoor pool, hot tub, and European dry sauna. Web site: www.bestwestern arizona.com.

Holiday Inn Canyon de Chelly, Indian Route 7, Chinle. Call 928-674-5000. Located on the site formerly occupied by Garcia's Trading Post, this hotel has a pool and restaurant, Garcia's, which serves American and Mexican cuisine. Rooms begin at $79/night. Web site: www.holidayinn .com.

Navajoland Inn & Suites, 392 W. AZ 264, St. Michaels. Call 928-871-5690. Web site: www.navajoland-innsuites .com.

Quality Inn Navajo Nation Capital, 48 W. AZ 264, Window Rock. Call 928-871-4108. Web site: www.qualityinn .com.

Thunderbird Lodge, inside Canyon de Chelly National Monument. Call 928-674-5841 or 1-800-679-2473. The 73 units of this motel-style lodge sit on the site of a trading post built in 1896. Winter rates range up to $95/night while summer rates top $150/night. Web site: www.tbirdlodge .com.

ATTRACTIONS AND RECREATION

Bowl Canyon Recreation Area. Call 928-871-6647. For fishing permits, call 928-871-6451. You can take a short detour off Indian Route 12 into the Bowl Canyon Recreation Area or continue approximately 9 miles to Camp Asáayi (*Ah-saa-yeh*) and nearby Asáayi Lake, where you can picnic, hike, canoe, and fish. Day use fee: $10/vehicle. Web site: www.navajo nationparks.org/htm/bowlcanyon.htm.

Canyon de Chelly National Monument, Indian Route 7, Chinle. Call 928-674-5500. You can view the canyon from its 10 designated overlooks—three along North Rim Drive and seven along South Rim Drive—for free. (The Navajo Parks and Recreation Department is considering charging an entrance fee in the near future.) Allow four hours to make all 10 stops. If you plan to hike to the White House Ruins, which is the only way you can enter the canyon without a Navajo guide, add an additional two hours to your visit. Jeep tours, guided hikes, and horseback excursions can be arranged through local hotels, but it's best to book these ahead of time since they can sell out, especially during the summer months. Web site: www.nps .gov/cach.

Ch'ihootso Indian Marketplace, corner of AZ 264 and Indian Route 12,

Window Rock. Call 928-871-5443. Shop for Navajo jewelry, crafts, and other treasures, and then enjoy a traditional Navajo meal from one of the market's indoor food stands.

Navajo Nation Council Chambers, Window Rock. Call 928-871-6417 for tour information. Eighty-eight council delegates representing 110 Navajo Nation chapters convene here four times a year. Tribal meetings are open to the public. When the council is not in session, tour the council chambers and view Navajo artist Gerald Nailor's murals, which depict Diné history and way of life.

Navajo Nation Museum, AZ 264, Window Rock. Call 928-871-7941. Part of the complex that includes a library and visitors center, the Navajo Nation Museum contains examples of Navajo arts and crafts along with a good exhibit on the Long Walk. Open Tuesday through Friday, 8–8, and Monday and Saturday, 8–5. Donations welcome.

Navajo Nation Zoological and Botanical Park, AZ 264 (behind the Navajo Nation Museum). Call 928-871-6574. Open daily 8–5, this small zoo showcases animals that are native to the Navajo Nation. Admission is free. Donations encouraged. Web site: www .navajozoo.org.

St. Michaels Museum, 24 Mission Road, St. Michaels. Call 928-871-4171. Established by Franciscan Friars in 1898, this mission now serves as a

museum. Open Monday through Friday, 9–5.

Window Rock Tribal Park, Window Rock. Call 928-871-6647. Open daily 8–5, this small park showcases the natural arch that gives the town its name. It also includes a veteran's memorial and a statute commemorating the service of the Navajo Code Talkers in World War II. Admission is free.

DINING

Changing Woman Café, Indian Route 7, inside Canyon de Chelly National Monument. Grab a cup of certified organic coffee at this small shop and peruse the paintings by Navajo artist Victoria Begay. Navajo music CDs and other gifts are on sale. Outdoor seating available.

Diné Restaurant, 48 W. AZ 264, Window Rock. As the restaurant attached to the Quality Inn Navajo Nation Capitol, Diné Restaurant delivers reliable cuisine that includes local favorites like mutton stew and Navajo tacos.

Garcia's Restaurant, Indian Route 7, Chinle. Next to the Holiday Inn Canyon de Chelly's lobby, Garcia's serves American, Southwestern, and Mexican fare. Open for breakfast, lunch, and dinner.

Junction Restaurant, 100 E. Main Street, Chinle. Part of the Best Western Canyon de Chelly Inn, this restaurant offers an extensive menu

Petroglyphs in Canyon de Chelly

that includes Navajo favorites like fry bread, mutton stew, and posole as well as stir fry and even Pizza Hut pizza. Open for breakfast, lunch, and dinner.

Thunderbird Cafeteria, Indian Route 7, inside Canyon de Chelly National Monument. Call 928-674-5841. Located in the old trading post at Thunderbird Lodge, this cafeteria-style restaurant serves Navajo dishes and Continental cuisine throughout the day. Looking for a souvenir? The Navajo rugs and artwork hanging on the walls are for sale. Web site: www.tbirdlodge.com.

GUIDES

Ancient Canyon Tours. Call 928-380-1563. In addition to 4x4 tours, you can arrange for hiking excursions and overnight camping through Ancient Canyon Tours. Web site: www.ancientcanyontours.com.

Canyon de Chelly Ancient Jeep Tours. Call 928-349-5912 to leave a message. Ride along in medicine man Oscar Bia's jeep as he points out the highlights of the canyon where he grew up. Web site: www.canyondechelly spiderrockjeeptour.com.

Canyon de Chelly Jeep Tour. Call 928-674-3772 or 1-877-343-3243. Authorized guides Leander Staley and DonVan Staley provide insightful jeep tours. Web site: www.acanyonde chellytour.com.

Canyon de Chelly Tours. Call 928-674-5433. From three-hour canyon tours to overnight adventures with storytelling, guide Leon Skyhorse Thomas provides the unique perspective of having assisted filmmakers on location in Navajoland.

Canyon Jeep Tours. Call 928-245-9592. Tours depart from the Holiday Inn parking lot at 9, 1, and 4. Call for reservations or schedule with the hotel's gift shop. Web site: www .canyonjeeptours.net.

Changing Woman Tours. Call 928-674-5260. Operating out of the Changing Woman Café, this company provides 4x4 tours, guided hikes, and camping trips. Web site: www .changingwomancafe.com.

Footpath Journeys. Call 928-724-3366. You can customize your visit to include hiking, horseback riding, overnight camping, and even an overnight stay in a hogan. Web site: www.footpathjourneys.com.

Thunderbird Lodge Tours. Call 928-674-5841. These group tours, offered at 9 and 1, traverse the canyon in an open-air Unimog and stop only at the White House and Antelope ruins. Rates begin at $52/adults and $40/children 12 and under. Web site: www.tbirdlodge.com.

Tseyi' Jeep Tours. Call 928-674-3262 or 928-349-5699. Navajo guide Bobby Vanwinkle Sr. offers hiking, camping, and jeep tours. Web site: www.tseyi jeeptour.com.

Totsonii Ranch. Call 928-220-5524. Navajo guides lead two-hour, four-hour, six-hour, and eight-hour horseback rides to Canyon de Chelly's ruins. Overnight trips are also available. Web site: www.totsoniiranch .com.

OTHER CONTACTS

Navajo Nation Hospitality Enterprise. Established by the Navajo Nation Tribal Council, the enterprise owns and operates the Quality Inn Navajo Nation (Tuba City), the Quality Inn Navajo Nation Capital (Window Rock), Quality Inn Lake Powell and the Navajo Travel Center. Its Web site provides visitor information on events, attractions, and Navajo culture. Web site: www.explorenavajo .com.

Navajo Nation Parks and Recreation, Bldg. 36A, AZ 264 and Indian Route 12, Window Rock. Call 928-871-6647. The parks and recreation department oversees the Navajo Nation's tribal parks including Monument Valley Tribal Park, Four Corners Monument, and Lake Powell Navajo Tribal Park. Find information online about the parks and events as well as permits and facility rentals. Web site: www .navajonationparks.org.

Navajo Nation Tourism Department. Call 928-871-6436. The tourism department can answer specific questions. For general information, check out DiscoverNavajo.com, the tourism department's online resource. You'll find itineraries, maps, lodging suggestions, and cultural information here. Web site: www.discovernavajo .com.

Painted Cliffs Welcome Center, I-40, Exit 359/Grants Road, Lupton. Call 928-688-2448. Open daily 8–5, the welcome center offers free maps and brochures to visitors and houses a notable collection of regional jewelry, pottery, and rugs. There's also a media room featuring 35 videos of Arizona attractions and 24-hour public restrooms.

8 The Hopi Way of Life

Estimated length: 83 miles to Keams Canyon

Estimated time: 1.5 hours

Getting there: From Flagstaff, take I-40 east. Follow the signs at Exit 201 for US 89 north. Continue for 65 miles to US 160. Turn right and head toward Tuba City, 10 miles east. The drive begins at the intersection of US 160 and AZ 264.

Highlights: Tour Hopi villages, eat a traditional meal, and shop for authentic arts and crafts. If you hire a Hopi guide, you'll gain access to much more, like Prophesy Rock, Coal Mine Canyon, and Taawa Petroglyph Area. Who knows? You may even be invited into a Hopi home or to watch a ceremonial dance.

To get to the Hopi Reservation, you have to first drive through the Navajo Reservation; Hopiland is completely surrounded by Navajo lands. From US 89, turn right toward Tuba City. On the left, you'll pass the Dinosaur Tracks, a Navajo-managed attraction (see Chapter 9 for more information), and as you go farther, you'll begin to notice a few scattered homes, the first signs Tuba City.

Mormons settlers founded Tuba City in the 1872 but had been present among the Hopi since Jacob Hamblin arrived in the 1850s. Hamblin and other missionaries introduced Mormonism, and while some were open to these outsiders, others were not. Over time, this caused a rift, which may have led Hopi chief Tuuvi' to leave Oraibi and settle permanently in the seasonal farming village of Moenkopi. In 1870, Hamblin invited Tuuvi' and his wife to Salt Lake City, and when the chief returned, he reciprocated, inviting the Mormons to live next to him at Moenkopi. They named their settlement Tuuvi' City, but it would eventually come to be known as Tuba City.

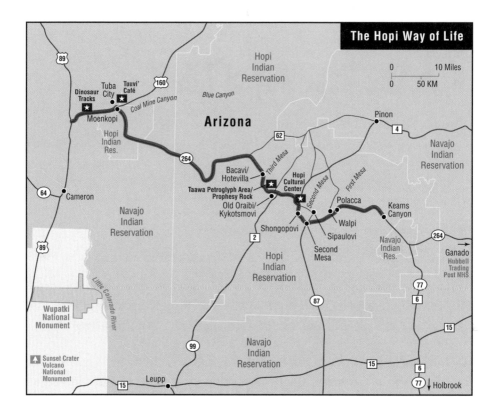

The village of Moenkopi and Tuba City still coexist. However, the former split in two: Upper and Lower Moenkopi. While Lower Moenkopi remains the traditional farming community in the Moenkopi Wash, Upper Moenkopi resides on the boundary of Tuba City. The Hopi in Upper Moenkopi tend to be more progressive and open to visitors, much like their ancestors tended to welcome the Mormons.

In Tuba City today, you find yourself caught between two worlds with US 160 as the border. To your right is Upper Moenkopi; to your left are Navajo shops, schools, hotels, restaurants, and homes. When President Chester Arthur signed an executive order in 1882 creating the Hopi Reservation, the United States government distrusted the Mormons and their alliance with the Hopi. By surrounding the Hopi Reservation with the Navajo Nation, the government hoped to force the Mormons, who had a hostile relationship with the Navajo, out of Hopiland. It worked.

Since this drive relates to the Hopi people and their culture, focus on the right

WHAT TIME IS IT?

While Arizona does not participate in daylight-saving time, the Navajo Nation does—7 AM in Flagstaff is 8 AM in Tuba City during the summer. That is unless you're on the Hopi side of the road. The Hopi Reservation follows Arizona's lead and does not adhere to daylight time. So, if you start from Flagstaff and cross Hopiland during the summer, you'll cross three time zones (sort of). It shouldn't matter much unless you schedule tours. Clarify with your guide when and where you're meeting, and you should be fine.

side of the road as you enter Tuba City, where you'll immediately notice the **Tuuvi' Travel Center**. Part gas station, part convenience store, and part restaurant, it is worth a stop for a couple of reasons. First, you'll need gas; make sure you have a full tank before heading out. Second, you can get maps and directions here. And lastly, you can sample Hopi foods at the **Tuuvi' Café**. Try the blue corn fry bread.

A Hopi dancer, *left*, and a Hopi musician, *right*, perform at the Moenkopi Legacy Inn & Suites.

WHAT'S FOR LUNCH?

Some tour guides offer a lunch option, allowing you to eat a traditional meal in a Hopi home for a reasonable fee. So, what can you expect? Mostly likely, you'll be served a mutton stew very similar to the version you can order at the Hopi Cultural Center or the Tuuvi' Café. Accompaniments might include thick bread rolls or piki, the paper-thin bread made from blue corn meal. Look for a sweetened corn dish, like blue corn tamales, to be on the table as well. Hopi tea, an orange-hued herbal tea, will probably round out your meal.

Piki bread is a traditional Hopi staple.

The travel center is located at the corner of US 160 and AZ 264. Across the street on AZ 264, you'll see the Moenkopi Legacy Inn & Suites, the first hotel to be built on the Hopi Reservation in 50 years. It also serves as the gateway to Hopiland, literally and figuratively. Every month, the hotel hosts the Natwani Coalition Agricultural Conference, which brings together Hopi speakers, artisans, and performers for an educational program. Sample Hopi foods, watch a ceremonial dance, and learn how to weave a Second Mesa basket. You can also arrange for tours of Hopiland through the Moenkopi Legacy Inn. Ask at the front desk.

Before striking out, consider what type of experience you want. You can explore the area without a guide, but you will be limited to the Hopi Cultural Center, artists' shops along the way, and village tours at Sipaulovi and Walpi. On the other hand, if you hire a Hopi guide, you gain access to Coalmine Canyon, the

Hopi Prophesy Rock, Taawa Petroglyph Area (also Dawa Park), and more.
I recommend hiring a guide, something
you can do at the Moenkopi Legacy Inn
or ahead of time by contacting the
guides listed at the end of this chapter.
You will see more and come away with
a deeper understanding of the Hopi
people and their culture.

Also, before going any farther, put
away all cameras, video cameras, cell
phones, pen and paper, sketchbooks,
voice recorders, or anything that could
be used in any way to record your visit.
Don't test this. You could lose your
camera or cell phone, permanently.

From the corner of US 60 and AZ
264, head east where, on the right,
Lower Moenkopi will appear. You can
enter the village, but unless you have a
guide or a specific reason to be there,

Baskets made by Hopi weavers

continue east to the villages of Sipaulovi or Walpi, both of which offer tours.
Lower Moenkopi is a more traditional village and hasn't embraced tourism to the
extent some of the others have, so there isn't as much to do or see here. Should
you decide to enter Lower Moenkopi anyway, follow all posted rules and immediately check in at the village visitor center.

One of the hidden wonders of Hopiland comes roughly 15 miles into the drive.
The red mudstone and white bleached rock of Coal Mine Canyon can be
glimpsed from the road if you know where to look, but you'll have to take an unmarked dirt road cutting north to actually stand on the rim. And that's not going
to happen without a Hopi guide. Not only is the road difficult to find, but visitors
can be fined for exploring on their own in undesignated areas. Go with a guide.
Hiking excursions into Coal Mine Canyon and the adjacent Blue Canyon can
also be arranged.

A guide can also take you to the Taawa Petroglyph Area, where more than

Coal Mine Canyon

You'll need a guide to see Taawa Petroglyph Area.

10,000 petroglyphs cover 40 rock wall panels. You could easily spend two hours here, walking along the sandstone walls as your Hopi guide explains the meaning behind the drawings. Equally impressive is the nearby Prophesy Rock. The petroglyphs on the door-sized boulder depict the coming of the Anglo settlers, two separate paths or lifestyles, and a judgment day. Hopis have several interpretations for these petroglyphs, so ask your guide about the different versions.

Hopi villages are divided between three mesas. As you travel east from Tuba City, you come to the Third Mesa first and the villages of Bacavi and Hotevilla. Like Moenkopi and Tuba City, the story of these villages begins with dissention when the village leaders in Old Oraibi decided to send their children to school and accept some of the Anglo ways. Hopi that wanted to adhere to more traditional ways left and founded Hotevilla, but conditions there became severe. Hoping for reconciliation, a small group returned to Old Oraibi, only to find they were no longer welcome. This band of Hopi then started Bacavi. You can visit these villages near Milemarker 367 on a tour with a Hopi guide.

Five miles down the road, you'll find the turnoff for Old Oraibi, which

The Hopi Cultural Center is located about halfway through the reservation.

dates back to 1150 A.D. and is considered by some to be the oldest continuously inhabited community in the United States. You can tour the village on your own—be sure to check in first—but again, it is best to go with a guide who can provide historical and cultural insight. While there, you may be approached by women and children to buy piki, the paper-thin, blue corn bread shaped like a rolled-up newspaper. Or you may be invited to an artist's home to see the crafts they have for sale.

Kykotsmovi, or New Oraibi, will be on your right just a few miles down the road. Found in the 1890 by villagers that wanted to be closer to the trading post and school, Kykotsmovi is the seat of the modern Hopi government. Between this point and the Hopi Cultural Center at Milemarker 379, you cross the boundary from First Mesa into Second Mesa.

The Hopi Cultural Center is on the left, about an hour east of Tuba City. Stop here to use the restrooms or stretch your legs. Inside, grab a bite to eat at the restaurant where you can order traditional Hopi foods like *tsilöngava* (chile

NOT JUST SEEDS IN THE GROUND

To the Hopi, farming is just as much a spiritual exercise as an agricultural one. In a land where the average yearly rainfall is about 12 inches or less, it takes keen observation, faith, and a "heart full of prayer" to yield successful crops of corn, beans, squash, melons, and fruits.

Fathers and uncles pass on traditional methods of farming to the next generation. These methods are considered a sacred knowledge, a connection to the Creator. Agriculture is so significant to the Hopi that it marks their calendar and influences how cultural activities are structured.

beans), *nöqkwivi* (hominy stew) and fry bread made with blue corn flour. A museum and motel are also onsite, and Native American vendors sell their crafts in the parking lot. During the summer, if you look across the street, you might see the Spirit Grille, a tented restaurant serving hamburgers.

At Milemarker 380, pull into the Talahaftewa Gallery, where Hopi jeweler and owner Ray Talahaftewa displays his workmanship and the crafts of other artists. Talahaftewa Gallery is one of the many artists' shops and galleries that line AZ 264 from Hotevilla to Keams Canyon. Watch also for Tsakurshovi, located approximately 1.5 miles east of the Hopi Cultural Center. This small store showcases the work of local Hopi artists and stocks traditional ceremonial items like gourds, furs, and moccasins. Have questions about the artists, the Hopi people, or anything you've seen? Owners Joseph and Janice Day will gladly answer them.

The drive continues past the village of Shungopavi. Look for the Second Mesa Day School on your right about 4 miles past the Hopi Cultural Center. Across the street, you'll see a paved road along the side of the Texaco gas station. Turn left. Behind the Texaco, near the mesa's base, you can see what remains of the former day school, clinic, and government buildings as you wind your way up to the village of Sipaulovi. When you get there, park near the Sipaulovi Visitor Center.

Sipaulovi means "the place of the mosquito" and actually refers to Homol'ovi, the area near Winslow that villagers fled to escape the mosquitoes of the Little Colorado River. You'll learn this, how the Sun Forehead and Bear clans founded Sipaulovi, and much else about the village's 300-year history in a 30-minute orientation video. Then guides escort you to the plaza, the rectangular space in the center of the village where the dances and ceremonies take place. Along the way, you'll meet craftsmen, and your guide will draw your attention to points of interest, like the other villages in the distance and the ancient footpaths connecting them. Tours are held Monday through Friday, 9–4.

Returning to AZ 264, turn left. Less than a mile down the road, you'll come to the intersection of AZ 87. Although this drive through the Hopi villages continues on AZ 264, if you headed south on AZ 87, you'd end up at the Homol'ovi State Park near Winslow.

Walpi Village offers a village experience similar to Sipaulovi's. Located on the First Mesa, it sits above the villages of Polacca and Hano. To get there, turn left at Milemarker 392. Signs will direct you to turn right and take the winding road to the top of the meas. Note, however, that Walpi is only accessible by passenger vehicles. RVs and trailers must be parked at the bottom of the mesa because there is no space to maneuver large or long vehicles in the village. In general, this applies to all villages: don't try to drive RVs and trailers into the actual villages.

When you arrive at Walpi, check in at Ponsi Hall. After a 20-minute video, you'll be taken on a walking tour of the village, including the plaza. Even though tours are normally offered Monday through Saturday, 9–3:30, you have no guarantees when you arrive. The day I visited, the village was closed to the public for a funeral. But you are just as likely to arrive on a feast day and be invited to view the dancing in the plaza. Villages do not post information online about closures or dances, so it really is the luck of the draw.

There will likely be artists selling pottery, kachina dolls, and piki bread. Although they are willing to negotiate, I've never felt pressured into making an unwanted purchase. The artists have always been friendly, polite, and willing to answer questions about their craft. Remember that arts and crafts are the primary source of income for many of these families and seriously consider making a purchase.

Eleven miles east of Polacca, the drive ends at Keams Canyon. Named for Indian agent Thomas Keam, the community has little to offer visitors. If you do find yourself in Keams Canyon, check behind the Bureau of Indian Affairs building where you'll find an inscription made by Kit Carson.

From Keams Canyon, you can continue to on to Ganado and the Hubbell Trading Post, to Canyon de Chelly or to Holbrook, via AZ 77.

IN THE AREA

ACCOMMODATIONS

Hopi Cultural Center, located near Milemarker 379 on AZ 264, Second Mesa. Call 928-734-2401. The cultural center has a 30-room hotel with basic but comfortable accommodations. Winter rates begin at $75/night, with summer rates beginning at $95/night. Web site: www.hopiculturalcenter.com

Moenkopi Legacy Inn & Suites, corner of US 160 and AZ 264. Call 928-283-4500. The first hotel built on the reservation in more than 50 years, Moenkopi Legacy Inn serves as the ideal base for exploring Hopiland. Rates start as low as $105/night. Web site: www.experiencehopi.com/hotel.

Quality Inn Navajo Nation, 10 N. Main Street, Tuba City. Call 928-283-4545. Located in Tuba City next to the Hogan Restaurant, this hotel also provides full RV hook-ups and six tent sites. Web site: www.qualityinn.com.

ATTRACTIONS AND RECREATION

Blue Canyon, Third Mesa. Hike this canyon, just northeast of Coal Mine Canyon, with a guide.

Coalmine Canyon, Third Mesa. You can hike with a guide or just photograph the red mudstone and bleached white rock canyon walls streaked with coal.

Hopi Cultural Center, located near Milemarker 379 on AZ 264, Second Mesa. Call 928-734-2401. The cultural center includes a restaurant, hotel, and small Hopi museum. Restroom facilities are also available here.

Old Oraibi, Milemarker 371, Third Mesa. You can tour the village—considered by the Hopi to be the oldest continuously inhabited community in the United States—on your own, but to make the most of your visit, arrange for a Hopi guide to lead you on a 30-minute or hour-long tour.

Corn is an important part of the Hopi way of life.

Prophesy Rock. You need a guide to see these petroglyphs which, according to some accounts, foretell a judgment day and the end of the world.

Sipaulovi Village, Second Mesa. Call 928-737-5426. After a 30-minute video, guides escort you on a one-hour tour of the 300-year-old village. Park at the visitor center. Fee: $15/adults, $12/seniors, and $8/youth. Tours are held Monday through Friday, 9–4. Web site: www.Sipaulovi HopiInformation.org.

Talahaftewa Gallery, Milemarker 380, Second Mesa. Call 928-734-9262.

Owner Ray Talahaftewa displays his renowned jewelry for sale as well as watercolor paintings and clay pottery. Open Monday through Friday, 9–5.

Taawa Petroglyph Area (Also Dawa Park). You need a guide to get to this site where more than 10,000 petroglyphs cover canyon walls.

Tsakurshovi, on AZ 264. This small shop offers the best of local Hopi artists and craftsmen and also supplies Hopis with traditional items like gourds, furs, and moccasins.

Walpi Village, First Mesa. Call 928-737-2670. On the one-hour walking tour of Walpi, you'll learn about the history, culture, and traditions of the village's people and meet with local artists. Tours are offered Monday through Saturday, 9–3:30 (the last tour begins at 3) and costs $13/person. No RVs or large vehicles are permitted in the village.

DINING

Hogan Restaurant, Main Street and Moenave Road. Call 928-283-5260. The menu includes pizza, hamburgers, and burritos as well as Navajo tacos and other Native American dishes. There's also a salad bar. Open daily for breakfast, lunch, and dinner.

Restaurant at the Hopi Cultural Center, located near Milemarker 379 on SR 264, Second Mesa. Call 928-734-2402. You'll find Hopi foods like *tsilöngava* (chile beans), *nöqkwivi* (hominy stew), and fry bread tacos on the menu, along with contemporary favorites like hamburgers. Try the blue fry bread made with blue corn flour. Open daily for breakfast, lunch, and dinner. Web site: www.hopi culturalcenter.com.

Spirit Grille, across from the Hopi Cultural Center on AZ 264. Open during the summer months, this roadside tent specializes in hamburgers and is popular with locals and tourists alike.

Tuuvi' Café, corner of US 160 and AZ 264, Tuba City. Call 928-283-4374. Located inside the Tuuvi' Travel Center, this café serves hamburgers, sandwiches, and fry bread, plus a full breakfast menu. Open daily 6–9.

GUIDES

Ancient Pathways Tours. Call 928-797-8145. Bertram Tsavadawa, a member of the Corn Clan, takes visitors on one-hour, half-day, and full-day tours of Hopiland. Each option includes a tour of Old Oraibi, the village where he grew up.

Evelyn Fredericks. Call 928-255-2112. Hopi sculptor Evelyn Fredericks leads customized tours.

Hopi Tours. Call 928-206-7433. Hopi anthropologist Micah Loma'omvaya shares the history, culture, arts and crafts, language, and traditions of his people through his tours. Lunch with a Hopi family can be arranged for an additional fee. Web site: www.hopi tours.com.

Left-Handed Hunter Tour Company. Call 928-206-7928. Both full-day and half-day tours with Gary Tso include Taawaki Petroglyph Site (another name for Tawa Petroglyph Area/Dawa Park), local villages, and Hopi artists' workshops.

Sacred Travel & Images. Call 928-734-6699. Take a full-day tour or chose to visit Third Mesa, First Mesa, or Tawa Petroglyph Area (also Dawa Park) separately.

OTHER CONTACTS

Experience Hopi. This online resource provides travel information, including maps, and lists authorized Hopi guides. Web site: www .experiencehopi.com.

Tuuvi' Travel Center, corner of US 160 and AZ 264. Named for Tuuvi', the first leader of Moenkopi, the travel center serves as a gateway to Hopiland. Fill up your tank at the gas station, grab a bite to eat at the Tuuvi' Café, or buy a souvenir. Maps and travel information are also available here.

A Navajo dancer performs in Monument Valley Navajo Tribal Park.

9 Scenes from the Old West

Estimated length: 105 miles to Monument Valley

Estimated time: 2 hours to Monument Valley

Getting there: From Flagstaff, take I-40 east. Follow the signs at Exit 201 for US 89 north. Continue for 65 miles to US 160. From Albuquerque, take I-40 west to Exit 201 and head north on US 89.

Highlights: Stand where dinosaurs once roamed, shop at authentic trading posts, learn about the Navajo Code Talkers at three museums, and take a jeep tour through Monument Valley. Movie lovers can try to spot where classics like *The Searchers, She Wore a Yellow Ribbon, Forrest Gump,* and *National Lampoon's Vacation* were filmed.

On this drive, you begin to get a sense of just how large the Navajo Nation is. Covering more than 27,000 square miles of Arizona, Utah, and New Mexico, the reservation extends north 70 miles on US 89 to Page while roughly following I-40 to the south. It includes Canyon de Chelly, Chaco Canyon, Lake Powell, and Monument Valley. And, near Tuba City, it surrounds another reservation: Hopiland.

As you turn onto US 160 from US 89, you cross into the Painted Desert, a multi-hued ribbon of sandstone, clay, and volcanic soils that extends from Marble Canyon south to I-40 near Winslow. This area was the site of an ancient lake during the Jurassic period, and fossilized dinosaur bones, eggs, and tracks can be found in the area. Watch for the sign between Milemarker 316 and 317 directing you to the Dinosaur Tracks on the left.

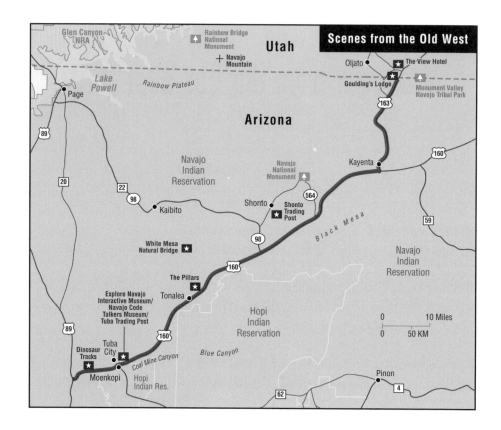

There's technically no charge to view the dinosaur tracks and fossils, but before you even park, a Navajo guide will approach your car and tell you where to meet him for a tour. Money is usually not discussed until after you've been led across the uneven rock surface, watching the guide squirt water into three-toed indentations and around the uneven, bony shapes. Then, you will be expected to tip your guide.

What should you tip? That's a difficult question to answer because there isn't a set tour. Your guide may spend 15 minutes with you or a half hour. He may be knowledgeable or unable to answer the simplest question. Go with your gut, keeping in mind that this is how your guide makes his living.

Tuba City butts up against the Hopi community of Moenkopi. Anything on the right side of the road will be Hopi; everything on the left side of the road will be Navajo-owned. The Hopi originally invited Mormon settlers to live next to them in a community platted by Erastus Snow in 1878. However, the Mormons were pressured by the federal government to sell their homes and farms to the Navajo in 1903, after Tuba City became part of the Navajo Reservation.

In Tuba City, consider spending some time at the Explore Navajo Interac-

CHECK YOUR WATCH

The Navajo Nation observes daylight-saving time. During summer months, when it is 9 AM in Flagstaff, it's 10 AM on the reservation. Keep this in mind when scheduling tours and planning your day.

GETTING THERE

On your way from Flagstaff to Tuba City, you have the opportunity to explore ancient ruins, visit a trading post, and walk on the moon—well, sort of. As you head north out of Flagstaff on US 89, the Sinagua (*Sin-ah-wa*) village, Elden Pueblo, sits at the base of Mount Elden. You can take a self-guided tour of the knee- to waist-high walls of what is thought to be a 60–70 room site.

Twelve miles outside Flagstaff, turn into Sunset Crater Volcano National Monument. The Apollo astronauts trained here in preparation for walking on the moon, and although you are restricted to paths and designated areas, you can figuratively walk in their footsteps.

If you continue past the crater, the road will eventually lead you back to US 89, but about an hour into the drive you'll come to Wupataki National Monument. A paved, self-guided trail starts behind the visitor center and leads you past 800-year-old ruins.

Thirty-six miles north of the Wupataki, the Cameron Trading Post offers a break from the road. In addition to the general post stocked with snacks, T-shirts, and Native American crafts, Cameron offers AAA accommodations at its lodge.

The Explore Navajo Interactive Museum

tive Museum. Created as an exhibit for the 2002 Winter Olympics in Salt Lake City, these displays found a home in a 7,000-square-foot, hogan-shaped museum behind the Tuba Trading Post. At $9/adult, it is pricey, and whether or not it's worth the cost of admission depends on what type of experience you expect. If you want to touch artifacts, examine objects under a microscope, try your hand at crafts, or view historical vignettes, you'll be disappointed. This museum is more academic. After a 10-minute video detailing the Navajo creation, you'll spend your time reading panels and watching videotaped tribe members talk about different aspects of Navajo life.

However, admission to the Navajo Code Talkers Museum, located in the back of the trading post, is included with the museum fee. It's probably best to ask the trading post clerk before you head into the museum since a chime sounds as you step through the door. And, yes, you do go through the doorway in the back marked DO NOT ENTER. While the museum is small, it does display the uniforms, weapons, and equipment used by the Navajo code talkers and their Japanese counterparts.

The Tuba Trading Post is a good place to shop for T-shirts, coffee mugs, Native American–themed DVDs, and Southwestern souvenirs, as well as authentic Navajo rugs, sand paintings, kachinas, and silver jewelry. Opened in 1870 by Charles Algert, the post was sold to the Babbitt Brothers 32 years later. To get an idea of how the historic post might have looked then, visit the trading post's grocery store by going through the side door off Moenave Street.

From Tuba City, take US 160 north toward Kayenta. About 5 miles outside of town, the Rare Metals Uranium Mill processed yellow cake uranium ore until in 1968. To the right, you can see where the United States Department of Energy gathered the low-level radioactive waste left behind and covered it with gray rocks. The Environmental Protection Agency continues to monitor how much, if any, uranium has seeped into the water and ground here.

The Navajo Code Talkers Museum is located in the back of the Tuba Trading Post.

THE UNBREAKABLE CODE

In the early months of World War II, Japanese intelligence broke every code the United States devised and, using fluent English speakers, they were able to sabotage messages and issue false commands that ambushed Allied troops. Military leaders realized they needed a better option and turned to Navajo, a language that had no alphabet and was almost impossible to master without early exposure.

The Navajo Code Talker program began in 1942 with 29 men who applied Navajo words to military terms. For example, the Navajo word for *turtle* represented a tank; likewise, the Navajo word for *chicken hawk* represented a dive bomber. They began with 200 terms. By the end of the war, the Code had grown to more than 600.

Japanese intelligence experts never cracked the code. It is considered the most ingenious and successful code in military history and is credited with saving countless lives.

The drive continues through a flat desert landscape for the next 20 miles on the way into the small communities of Tonalea and adjoining Red Lake. In 1878, George Washington McAdams established a local trading post, which was eventually sold to Sam Dittenhoffer, a German merchant. To stock the post, Dittenhoffer became heavily indebted to the Babbitt Brothers, and when he died at the

hands of a jealous rival for the affections of a young Flagstaff woman, the Babbitts assumed control of the trading post. The Red Lake Trading Post is the first of many the Babbitts would go on to own.

One mile north, look to the left side of the road where you'll see the sandstone formations known as Elephant Feet or Elephant Legs. The Spanish called these features *Los Pilares* or The Pillars. Pull off to the left for a fun photo op with family or friends.

For the next hour, you can appreciate the landscape stretching before you. On your right, you'll see Black Mesa or *Dzitíjiin* in Navajo, meaning "black mountain." The highland plateau extends from Red Lake, past Kayenta and around to Chinle; it gets its dark appearance from the presence of coal. Peabody Energy has mined coal here since the 1960s, angering many Navajo and Hopi who believe the mine's slurry pipeline depletes the groundwater they need for their farms and livestock.

As you drive, you'll pass turnoffs to two points of interest. The first, AZ 98, takes you to the small community of Shonto and its historic trading post, the **Shonto Trading Post.** Beyond that, you'll reach Antelope Canyon, Antelope Point Marina and Lake Powell. If you turn onto AZ 564 and drive 10 miles, you'll end up at **Navajo National Monument** and its three intact cliff dwellings.

There's no charge to visit the Ancestral Puebloan ruins of Navajo National Monument. Behind the visitor center, three short trails lead to overlooks. The 1-mile roundtrip Sandal Trail gives you a good view of the Betatakin cliff dwelling while the Aspen Trail branches off, descending 300, feet for a view of the ancient aspen forest. Canyon View Trail provides a view of Betatakin Canyon. Longer, more strenuous hikes to the Betatakin ruins leave twice a day from the visitor center. During the summer, rangers also lead a 17-mile roundtrip hike to Keet Seel, the ruins discovered by Richard Wetherill while he was searching for a lost mule. Reservations are required.

Kayenta lies south of Monument Valley, at the junction of US 160 and US 163. While in town, stop by the **Burger King,** where you'll find an impressive Navajo Code Talkers display tucked among the booths. Most of the artifacts—photographs, documents, helmets, flags, and firearms—belonged to King Mike, owner Richard Mike's father, who served as a private first class in the South Pacific during World War II. The younger Mike claims that Kayenta has more Navajo Code Talker memorabilia than the Pentagon, and he plans to one day open a museum next to the Burger King to showcase the rest of his father's collection.

To get to **Monument Valley Navajo Tribal Park**, turn left onto US 163. Signs will direct you to turn right at the park's entrance 20 miles north of Kayenta, just across the Utah border, where you'll pay the $5/person entrance fee (children under 9 are free). From here, proceed to the visitor center, located next to **The View Hotel**. There's a good museum here that displays Navajo artifacts, clothing

Navajo exhibits on display at The View Hotel

and crafts, and the room to the right of the museum contains photographs of the Navajo Code Talkers. Both are free.

Monument Valley contains some of the most recognizable natural geological formations in the world, thanks in large part to Hollywood. Legendary director John Ford partnered with John Wayne to film *Stagecoach, She Wore a Yellow Ribbon,* and *The Searchers* here. Forest Gump ends his cross-country run *(Forest Gump),* the Griswolds' station wagon falls apart *(National Lampoon's Vacation),* and Marty McFly time travels to 1885 from a drive-in theater *(Back to the Future III),* all in Monument Valley. Before you leave the visitor center, survey the area from the observation point near the museum's entrance. You'll probably recognize the mesas and buttes before you.

As you embark on the self-guided, 17-mile scenic drive, you descend to what was the floor of a vast inland sea during the Cenozoic era. When the waters receded, they left behind beds of compacted sand some hundreds of feet thick. Over time, wind sculpted these sandstones, creating the incredible landscape you see. The self-guided drive winds through several of the park's highlights, but to get the most out of your visit, hire a guide. Tour guides can provide geological information, cultural insight, and historical perspective. Plus, they can take you to areas few people see.

The Mittens at Monument Valley Navajo Tribal Park

The view from John Ford's Point

With or without a guide, your first stop will overlook the **East and West Mitten Buttes**. Although these formations look like hands, the Navajo believe these formations are spiritual beings that watch over them. Behind you are **Merrick Butte** and **Mitchell Mesa**, named for two prospectors who discovered silver in the valley. Legend has it that Navajo warriors warned the two that if they returned to claim anymore silver, they'd be killed. James Merrick and Ernest Mitchell succumbed to the temptation and paid with their lives, ironically at the hands of either Utes or Paiutes and not Navajos. They died near the formations that bear their names.

You pass **Elephant Butte** and **The Three Sisters** on your way to **John Ford's Point**, one of the director's favorite locations within the park. Navajo vendors sell their crafts, and for a few dollars you can take a photograph of a Navajo boy on a horse at the point's edge. It's the last stop many visitors make in the park since the dirt road looping around Camel Butte can require four-wheel drive in spots.

A trip to Monument Valley wouldn't be complete without a visit to **Gould-**

Petroglyphs in Monument Valley

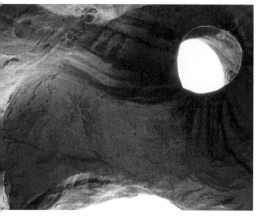

This rock formation in Monument Valley resembles an eagle.

ing's Lodge, located across from the tribal park entrance, on the other side of US 163. Harry Goulding first glimpsed Monument Valley as a sheepherder in 1923 and saw potential for the remote area. In October 1925, he founded Goulding's Trading Post with his wife, Mike. Fourteen years later, when Goulding learned that a Hollywood studio was looking for a Southwestern setting for a major production, he pressed his friend, photographer Josef Muench, to make a booklet of prints featuring Monument Valley's iconic images. Those photographs persuaded John Ford to film *Stagecoach* here.

Goulding's maintains an interesting museum in what used to be the original trading post. As you enter, you'll see the post much as it looked 100 years ago. Canned goods, Navajo crafts, guns, bags of raw wool, and other items are on display. An old ledger and the original scales are particularly interesting. The Josef Muench Room showcases Muench's photographs, while the Movie Room pays tribute to Hollywood's work in the valley. Upstairs, you can view the Living Quarters, which appears much as it would have during the late 1940s.

Before you leave, walk behind the museum to Captain Nathan Brittles's Cabin. The small building was actually the potato cellar where Mike stored her fresh fruits and vegetables, but for the movie *She Wore a Yellow Ribbon,* it served as the personal quarters of John Wayne's character, at least the exterior did. All interior shots were filmed on a Hollywood soundstage.

IN THE AREA

ACCOMMODATIONS

Best Western Wetherill Inn, 1000 Main Street, Kayenta. Call 928-697-3231. Clean, moderately priced accommodations a short drive from Monument Valley.

FireTree Bed & Breakfast, located off US 163 (see online printed map for exact location), Monument Valley. You'll sleep in a hogan at this unique bed & breakfast. Rates are $215/night for one or two guests, $30/night for each additional guest. Web site: www.firetreeinn.com.

Goulding's Lodge, 1000 Main St., Monument Valley, Utah. Call 435-727-3231. Home to John Wayne and John Ford during the filming of such classics as *Stagecoach* and *The Searchers*, Goulding's Lodge can accommodate guests in 62 standard, nonsmoking rooms. Larger suites, cabins, RV hook-ups, and campsites are also available. During your stay, you can rent copies of old Westerns filmed in the area to watch in your room, visit the onsite museum featuring movie memorabilia, and arrange a tour of Monument Valley Tribal Park. Rates are $25/night for campground. At the lodge, rates begin at $80/night during the winter and double that during the summer. Web site: www.gouldings.com.

An old wagon sits in front of Goulding's Lodge.

Hampton Inn of Kayenta, US 160, Kayenta. Call 928-697-3170. This three-story, adobe-style Hampton Inn offers affordable accommodations and a complimentary breakfast. Web site: www.hamptoninn.com.

Kayenta Monument Valley Inn, junction of US 160 and US 163. Call 928-697-3221. Formerly the Holiday Inn Kayenta, the Kayenta Monument Valley Inn has 164 rooms, including eight family suites. Try to book a room in the recently renovated portion of the hotel. Web site: www.kayentamonumentvalleyinn.com.

Moenkopi Legacy Inn & Suites, corner of US 160 and AZ 264. Call 928-283-4500. Although the accommodations are Hopi-inspired, this is the newest hotel in Tuba City. Rates start as low as $105/night. Web site: www.experiencehopi.com/hotel.

Quality Inn Navajo Nation, 10 N. Main Street, Tuba City. Call 928-283-4545. Located in Tuba City next to the Hogan Restaurant, this hotel also provides full RV hook-ups and six tent sites. Web site: www.qualityinn.com.

The View Hotel, located inside Monument Valley Tribal Park. Call 435-727-5555. Opened in December 2008, this Navajo-owned business is the only hotel located within Monument Valley Tribal Park. Each of the 95 rooms boasts a private, eastern-facing balcony with incredible views. If you're a photography enthusiast, book one of the StarView rooms on the top floor that allow you to take long exposure, night-time photographs of the valley from the comfort of your room. Web site: www.monumentvalleyview.com.

ATTRACTIONS AND RECREATION

Burger King Navajo Code Talkers Display, US 160, Kayenta. Call 928-697-3534. Order a burger and fries. Then check out the Navajo Code Talkers display featuring vintage posters, Japanese phrase books, and weaponry.

Dinosaur Tracks, between Milemarkers 316 and 317 on US 160. View Jurassic-era dinosaur tracks and fossilized bones. Technically, there is no fee, but you will be greeted by Navajo guides who expect payment for their tour. Web site: www.experiencehopi.com/dinotracks.html.

Monument Valley Navajo Tribal Park, AZ 163, Monument Valley. Call 435-727-5874. You can explore this iconic valley with a Navajo guide on a jeep tour, horseback ride, hot air balloon ride or hike. Although you can take a short self-guided tour, hiring a guide is the best way to see Monument Valley. They can take you farther into the park and provide insights into the Navajo people, culture, and history, as well as information about the forma-

THE SACRED MOUNTAINS

Navajo believe their Creator placed them between four sacred mountains and instructed them to never leave their sacred homeland. Those mountains are: Mount Blanco to the east, the San Francisco Peaks to the west, Mount Hesperus to the north, and Mount Taylor to the south.

tions you're seeing. At the visitors center, you'll also find a trading post with Native American crafts, film memorabilia, and souvenirs, as well as a small museum devoted to the Navajo people and to the Navajo Code Talkers. Open 7–7. The park fee is $5/person (free for kids under 9). Web site: www.navajonationparks .org. Highlights in the park include:

❖ **East and West Mitten:** These iconic buttes resemble hands or coffee pots, but the Navajo believe they signify deities watching over them.

❖ **Elephant Butte:** The name says it all.

❖ **John Ford's Point:** Named for the Hollywood director who worked with John Wayne on *Stagecoach* and *She Wore a Yellow Ribbon*.

❖ **Merrick Butte:** Prospector James

Merrick died near the butte that now bears his name.

❖ **Mitchell Mesa:** Merrick's partner, Ernest Mitchell, also died near Merrick Butte, but this mesa is named for him.

❖ **Rain God Mesa:** Navajo medicine men pray and give thanks to the Rain God here.

❖ **The Three Sisters:** This formation represents a Catholic nun facing her two pupils.

Navajo Code Talkers Museum, corner of Main Street and Moenave Road, in the back of the Historic Tuba City Trading Post, Tuba City. Small but good display of uniforms and equipment used by the code talkers and Japanese soldiers, along with black sand from Iowa Jima. Free with paid admission to the Navajo Interactive Museum next door.

Navajo Interactive Museum, corner of Main Street and Moenave Road, Tuba City. Call 623-412-0297. Located behind the Historic Tuba City Trading Post, this hogan-shaped museum displays exhibits created for the 2002 Winter Olympics in Salt Lake City. Informative? Yes. Interactive? Not so much, according to my 12-year-old, who breezed through the 7,000-square-foot museum in less than a half hour. Admission is a bit pricey for what you get, but it does include entrance to the Navajo Code Talkers Museum in the back of the trading post: $9/adults, $7/seniors, and

$6/children ages 7–12. Open Monday through Friday, 9–5, and Saturday, 9–9. Closed Sunday.

Navajo National Monument, AZ 564, Shonto. Call 928-672-2700. Three Ancestral Puebloan ruins make up this national monument: Betatakin Ruin, Inscription House, and Keet Seel. Short rim trails lead to overlooks. Longer hikes to Betatakin and Keet Seel are available daily through the summer. There is no fee to enter the park or participate in any of the hikes. The visitor center is open daily. Web site: www.nps.gov/nava.

Shonto Trading Post, 6 miles east of AZ 96, Shonto. Business is still conducted in the original building, erected shortly after World War I.

Tuba Trading Post, corner of Main Street and Moenave Road, Tuba City. In operation since 1870, this trading post has hosted Teddy Roosevelt and author Zane Grey. Today you'll find Native American crafts, books, CDs, souvenirs, and more. In the back, a hallway leads you to the Navajo Code Talkers Museum (see above).

DINING

Amigo Café, US 163, Kayenta. Call 928-697-8448. Good, reasonably priced Mexican food.

Blue Coffee Pot Restaurant, junction of US 160 and US 163. Diner fare with Navajo and American entrées. Open for breakfast, lunch, and dinner.

Golden Sands Café, US 163, Kayenta. This café delivers a tasty repertoire of local favorites like Navajo tacos and traditional fare like salad, burgers, and fried chicken.

Hogan Restaurant, 10 N. Main Street, Tuba City. Call 928-283-4545. Located next to the Navajo Interactive Museum, this restaurant offers Navajo, Mexican, and American entrées.

Pizza Edge, junction of US 160 and US 163, Kayenta. Call 928-697-8427. Don't judge a book by its cover. This place serves great pizza and milkshakes.

Reuben Heflin Restaurant, US 160, Kayenta. Call 928-697-3170. Located at the Hampton Inn of Kayenta, this restaurant serves Southwestern and Native American cuisine. Eat inside or outside on the patio. Open for dinner year-round and for lunch and dinner, March 15 until October 14.

Stagecoach Dining Room, 1000 Lodge Road, Monument Valley. Dine on traditional Navajo dishes or Southwestern favorites while taking in the view made famous by John Wayne, John Ford, and Henry Fonda in classic Hollywood Westerns. Part of Goulding's Lodge. Open for breakfast, lunch, and dinner.

The View Restaurant, located at The View Hotel, inside Monument Valley Tribal Park. Enjoy a menu featuring Navajo-inspired and American en-

Monument Valley Navajo Tribal Park

trées and the sounds of a local flutist while looking out over the iconic landscape of Monument Valley. Since this is the Navajo Nation, alcohol is not served. Open for breakfast, lunch, and dinner. Web site: www.monument valleyview.com/dining.

Wagon Wheel Restaurant, junction of US 160 and US 163, inside the Kayenta Monument Valley Inn. Call 928-697-3221. Native American and traditional American offerings. Kids eat free.

GUIDES

Bennett Guided Tours. Call 435-727-3283. Jeep tours through Monument Valley with options to take you off the beaten path.

Black's Tours. Call 928-429-0637. This

tour company offers jeep, horseback, and hiking tours with the option of an overnight stay in a hogan. You'll also enjoy storytelling and traditional songs. Web site: www.blacksmonumentvalleytours.com.

Blackwater Tours. Call 435-727-3312. Jeep tours. Full-moon excursions available. Web site: www.blackwatertours.com.

Crawley's Monument Valley Tours. Call 928-697-3463. Guides lead half-day, all-day, and sunset tours through Monument Valley in vehicles ranging from 8-passenger vans to 29-passenger minibuses. Web site: www.crawleytours.com.

Goulding's Monument Valley Tours. Call 435-727-3231. Group tours in an open-air vehicle. Hiking, all-day, and full-moon options are also available. Web site: www.gouldings.com/tours.

Kéyah Hóshóní. Call 928-309-7440. Offering vehicle tours, hikes, overnight camping, and photographic excursions in Monument Valley.

Monument Valley Tours. Call 435-727-3313. Several jeep tour options, including half-day and full-day tours, and cookouts. Web site: www.monumentvalleytours.net.

Sacred Mountain Tours. Call 435-727-3218. Guided jeep, hiking, and horseback riding tours. Web site: www.monumentvalley.net.

Simpson's Trailhandler Tours. Call 435-727-3362. Navajo guides conduct jeep tours, hikes, and photographic expeditions throughout Monument Valley. Traditional meals and an overnight stay in a hogan can be arranged. Web site: www.trailhandlertours.com.

OTHER CONTACTS

Kayenta Township, Kayenta. Call 928-697-8451. The township's Web site provides information on local dining, accommodations, and attractions. Web site: www.kayentatownship.net.

Navajo Nation Hospitality Enterprise. Established by the Navajo Nation Tribal Council, the enterprise owns and operates the Quality Inn Navajo Nation (Tuba City), the Quality Inn Navajo Nation Capital (Window Rock), Quality Inn Lake Powell, and the Navajo Travel Center. Its Web site provides visitor information on events, attractions and Navajo culture. Web site: www.explorenavajo.com.

Navajo Nation Parks and Recreation, Bldg. 36A at AZ 264 and Indian Route 12, Window Rock. Call 928-871-6647. The parks and recreation department oversees the Navajo Nation's tribal parks, including Monument Valley Tribal Park, Four Corners Monument, and Lake Powell Navajo Tribal Park. Find information online about the parks and events as well as permits

and facility rentals. Web site: www
.navajonationparks.org.

Navajo Nation Tourism Department.
Call 928-871-6436. The tourism department can answer specific questions. For general information, check
out DiscoverNavajo.com, the tourism
department's online resource. You'll

find itineraries, maps, lodging suggestions, and cultural information
here. Web site: www.discovernavajo
.com.

**Shepherd's Eyes Courtyard Visitor
Center,** Kayenta. Call 928-697-3368.
Area information and espresso bar.

The Navajo Bridge spans the Colorado River.

10 The Paiutes and Lees Ferry

Estimated length: 92 miles from Lees Ferry to Kanab

Estimated time: 1.5 hours to Kanab

Getting there: From Flagstaff, take 1-40 to US 89, Exit 201. Head north for two hours to the US 89A cutoff. From Albuquerque, head across to Exit 201 and take US 89 to US 89A.

Highlights: By starting in Page, you'll be able to tour the Glen Canyon Dam. From there, US 89A directs you past Lees Ferry, across the Navajo Bridge, and to Pipe Spring National Monument, where you'll find a historic Mormon ranch. Detours take you to the North Rim of the Grand Canyon and Kanab, nicknamed Little Hollywood for its role in movies like *Butch Cassidy and the Sundance Kid* and TV series like *Gunsmoke.*

In March 1864, Jacob Hamblin—the same pioneer that introduced Mormonism to the Hopi—made the first successful crossing of the Colorado River at the point that would become **Lees Ferry.** Hostilities between Mormon settlers and Navajo had escalated, and Hamblin was sent to warn the Navajo to stop stealing horses and raiding Mormon interests. But his warning went unheeded. In late 1869, the Mormons posted guards at the crossing and built a small outpost called Fort Meeks.

The following year, Mormon President Brigham Young excommunicated John D. Lee for Lee's role in the Mountain Meadows Massacre, which led to the deaths of 120 Arkansas emigrants. Instructing Lee to "make yourself scarce and keep out of the way," Young then exiled him to Fort Meeks to establish a ferry crossing. The first real ferryboat at Lees Ferry launched on January 11, 1873. Four years later,

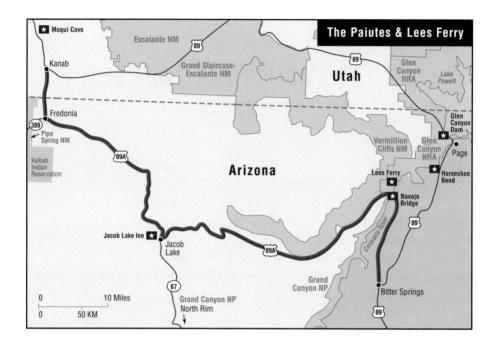

Lee would be tried and executed for the massacre. One of his wives, Emma, continued to operate the ferry until 1879, when the church realized the ferry's significance and purchased the rights from her.

As you approach Bitter Springs, where US 89A splits from US 89, you have a decision to make. The drive on 89A actually begins at this point, veering toward Lees Ferry, but to truly appreciate the **Glen Canyon National Recreational Area** where the historic ferry is located, consider staying on US 89 and driving 25 miles north to Page first. On the way, if you have time, stop at **Horseshoe Bend** and hike to the overlook where the Colorado River bends in a horseshoe shape. Go early, especially during the summer, and bring plenty of water.

Turn right at either South Lake Powell Boulevard or the next light, North Lake Powell Boulevard. You can't go wrong either way since the two form a loop through Page. While in town, visit the **John Wesley Powell Memorial Museum**. In 1869, Powell led nine men on a three-month exploration of the Colorado River and the Grand Canyon. At the museum, you'll see exhibits dedicated to his expedition, but you'll also find Native American and pioneer artifacts. The museum doubles as a visitor information center. Schedule a river trip here, arrange a tour of Antelope Canyon, or ask for lodging and restaurant recommendations.

From Page, continue a few miles north to the Glen Canyon Dam and the Carl Hayden Visitor Center. At the center, you'll learn about the dam's construction, and for $5, you can tour it. Don't miss the gigantic relief map that shows the entire recreational area, stretching from Lees Ferry to the Orange Cliffs of Utah. Several exhibits relate to local geography, geology, and history.

The 180-mile waterway is the second-largest man-made lake in the United States and one of the Southwest's most popular destinations for water sports. You can boat, ski, Jet Ski, tube, and fish. Houseboats are also available for rent at the Lake Powell and Antelope Point marinas, but if you'd rather stick to the shore, you can camp. On land, you can hike, mountain bike, and horseback ride.

At one time or another, the Southern Ute, Pauites, and Ancestral Puebloans all called the Glen Canyon National Recreational Area home; the Navajo still do. Backtracking to where US 89 splits from US 89A, you'll pass Navajo vendors selling their crafts. Pull over to browse the handmade jewelry, pottery, and other

US 89A heading towards Vermillion Cliffs

crafts for sale. You can usually negotiate with the artists, and whatever you pay will be much less than what the same piece would sell for at a trading post.

When you reach US 89A, head toward Lees Ferry and Jacob Lake. The road dips and curves gently for about 11 miles before you reach the Navajo Bridge. Cross it and park in the lot for the interpretive center. You can skip the center, which is nothing more than a park service gift shop; the bridge is the main attraction.

Built in 1929, the bridge bypassed Lees Ferry, which couldn't handle the increasing automobile traffic. Over the years, as automobiles grew bigger and heavier, passage on the 18-foot wide bridge became more and more dangerous. Construction began on a new bridge in May 1993 and was completed two years later. As you drive US 89A, you cross the second bridge. To your right, the original bridge remains open for pedestrian travel. From the parking lot, you can walk

RAFTING THE COLORADO

Most Colorado River rafting trips begin in the vicinity of Lees Ferry, so if you've ever dreamed of retracing at least a portion of John Wesley Powell's great expedition, book your trip before you leave home. Trips vary in length from 7 to 12 days depending on whether you opt to go by motorized pontoon, raft, or dory, and on how far you go (most trips take you about 188 of the entire 279 miles). A few local companies are listed below:

❖ **Colorado River Discovery,** 130 6th Avenue, Page. Call 928-645-9175 or 1-888-522-6644. Half-day, smooth-water rafting trips starting at the Glen Canyon Dam and ending at Lees Ferry. A full-day rowing option is available, too. Web site: www.raftthecanyon.com.

❖ **Hatch River Expeditions,** Marble Canyon. Call 1-800-856-8966. Bus Hatch led his first commercial rafting trip down through the Grand Canyon in 1934. His company has been taking adventurers on motorized, oar-powered, and kayak expeditions ever since. Web site: www.hatchriverexpeditions.com.

❖ **Wild River Adventures,** Page. Call 1-800-992-8022. Raft the Colorado River for 3.5 days up to 16 days. Motorized and oar options available. Web site: www.riveradventures.com.

The original Navajo Bridge, built in 1929, and its 1993 replacement

to the other side, where more Navajo vendors wait, and then back, taking in the Colorado River some 467 feet below.

Immediately after leaving the Navajo Bridge Interpretative Center, you'll see the turn for Lees Ferry. Take it. Less than a mile down the road, you come to a pay station on your right. You're on your honor to pull in and pay the $15/car entrance fee to the recreational area, something you won't need to do if you've visited Lake Powell and paid the fee already within the last seven days. As you drive the remaining 4 miles, you'll pass Cathedral Wash, a 1-mile hike through a narrow limestone passage. The formation, Balanced Rock, is just beyond that, on the left side of the road.

Fishing lures most visitors to the area. The waters 15.5 miles from the outflow of Glen Canyon Dam are a constant 48 degrees, the perfect environment for rainbow trout. You can hire a guide through companies like **Lees Ferry Anglers** in nearby Marble Canyon, or fish on your own.

THE MOST PHOTOGRAPHED SLOT CANYON IN THE SOUTHWEST

Whether you realize it or not, you've probably seen the orange sandstone walls of Antelope Canyon in a calendar or on an inspirational poster. Light cuts through the dim slot, illuminating stone surfaces shaped by wind, water, and time. The scene is both peaceful and awe-inspiring.

To visit, you'll need to hire a Navajo guide. You can make reservations online before you go through the Navajo Nation Parks & Recreation Web site, www.navajonationparks.org. Or you can hire one of the outfitters stationed along Lake Powell Boulevard. Another option is to drive directly to the canyon, located a few miles east of Page, just off US 98. Cost will be comparable no matter which option you choose: about $30/person to visit or $50/person for an extended stay of up to two hours to photograph the canyon.

Bring water, a camera, and a tripod if you own one. Sand blows across the top of the canyon and sprinkles down on anything and everything below, so you may also want to bring plastic bags and canned air to protect your camera and gear. Consider eye protection, like sunglasses, too. Get sand in your eyes, and you could wind up with a scratched cornea.

Lonely Dell Ranch, Lee's historic homestead, sits at the edge of the parking lot on Lees Ferry Road. A self-guided tour directs you past the ferry site, the fort, a bunkhouse, and the American Placer Corporation Office. Farther down the trail, you'll see the sunken remains of the corporation's steamboat, the *Charles H. Spencer,* in the Colorado River. Don't expect too much from this tour—the stone buildings are locked, and there are no exhibits or interpretive displays.

Return to US 89A, the original highway through the area. While construction of the Glen Canyon Dam was underway, the United States Department of Transportation completed a new highway running through Page, Arizona, to the dam, and into Utah. In 1966, US 89 replaced US 89A as the main route to Kanab, Utah, where the two merge. Along US 89A, you pass several small communities, which are really nothing more than a lodge, a restaurant, and maybe a gas station. The services at Lees Ferry are the last remnants of civilization until Jacob Lake, near the Grand Canyon's North Rim.

The Lonely Dell Ranch at Lees Ferry

The road roughly follows the base of the **Vermillion Cliffs National Monument** to your right. You can hike and camp in the national monument, but the ranger station, trailheads, and campsites are northwest of Page, in Utah, on US 89. As you drive, try to spot a California condor. Through a local reintroduction program, the condor population has exploded from 22 in 1982 to more than 200 today, with a quarter of those living in Arizona. A condor viewing area is located 2 miles off US 89A, on House Rock Valley Road.

Soon after you pass the turn for the condor viewing area, you enter the Kaibab National Forest and begin the climb to Jacob Lake. Named for Jacob Hamblin, the small community serves as the gateway to the Grand Canyon. There isn't much here at the intersection of US 89A and AZ 67 except the **Jacob Lake Inn**, a restaurant, a campground, and a gas station. If you turn left on AZ 67, it's approximately 45 miles to the North Rim of **Grand Canyon National Park**. A side trip into the park will add several hours, if not a full day, to your drive.

It takes about a half hour to get from Jacob Lake to Fredonia. Located on the Arizona-Utah border, Fredonia takes its name from the words *freedom* and *doña,* the Spanish word for wife, and refers to the community's settlement by Mormon polygamists seeking refuge from federal agents in 1885. A few antique and gift

A raft journeys past Lees Ferry on the Colorado River.

The Vermillion Cliffs

shops line the street as you approach AZ 389. Turn left and drive 15 miles to **Pipe Spring National Monument.**

Ancestral Puebloans first inhabited the area, followed by Southern Paiute Indians. In 1858, Hamblin, his traveling companions, and a Paiute guide, stopped for the night at the site Paiutes called *Matungwa'va*. The Mormons renamed the site Pipe Spring, and it gained a reputation with ranchers as a good campsite and watering hole. In 1863, James M. Whitmore purchased the 160 acres around Pipe Spring and established a ranch with approximately 400 longhorn and 1,000 sheep. However, while pursuing Paiutes who allegedly stole Pipe Springs cattle and sheep, Whitmore and his ranch hand were murdered three years later. After his death, Mormon leadership purchased the ranch from Whitmore's widow to establish a church ranch, and in 1872 they built a fort that became known as Winsor Castle.

US 89A continues past the Vermillion Cliffs towards the North Rim of the Grand Canyon.

WHO ARE THE PAIUTES?

Paiute means "true Ute" or "water Ute." Largely nomadic, at one time, the tribe extended from Oregon to Las Vegas and included parts of Arizona and Southern California. Today, the numerous bands are usually recognized as three groups: the Northern Paiutes, the Owens Valley Paiutes, and the Southern Paiutes.

When you visit the national monument, take the 30-minute tour of the fortified ranch house, but first spend some time in the visitor center. Exhibits feature information about the *E'nengweng*, the Paiutes' name for the Ancestral Puebloans who built a pueblo near Pipe Springs; the kahn or traditional Paiute dwelling made from trees and brush; and the Kaibab Paiute way of life. Another display explains the relationships among Paiute bands. The local Kaibab are only one of 16 Southern Paiute bands.

The drive ends in Kanab. From Pipe Springs, return to US 89A and continue north. Fredonia merges into Kanab, with the Utah border serving as the only real separation between the two. If you have time, plan to spend at least a day in Kanab, perhaps even extending your trip by visiting nearby Zion National Park, Bryce Canyon National Park, or Coral Pink Sand Dunes State Park.

The Frontier Movie Town and Little Hollywood Movie Museum in Kanab, Utah

Kanab was often referred to as Little Hollywood during the 1930s. Over the years, celebrities like Tom Mix, Maureen O'Hara, Frank Sinatra, Dean Martin, and Sammy Davis Jr. starred in productions filmed in the area, but it is perhaps best known as the setting for

The scenery changes near the North Rim of the Grand Canyon.

Moqui Cave displays Native American artifacts.

early scenes in *Butch Cassidy and the Sundance Kid,* starring Paul Newman and Robert Redford. Television also used the Kanab area as a backdrop for several series, including *Gunsmoke, Have Gun Will Travel,* and *Death Valley Days.* You can learn more about Kanab's starring role in movies and TV at Frontier Movie Town and Little Hollywood Movie Museum. The free attraction features a Western movie set.

For a change of pace, visit the Best Friends Animal Sanctuary. Nearly 2,000 dogs, cats, horses, pigs, and other animals live at the sanctuary, sent here for special care from shelters and rescue groups throughout the country. While many of the animals are adoptable, some are too traumatized, old, or handicapped for placement. The sanctuary provides a permanent home for them. You can tour the facility and even volunteer your time.

Before you leave the area, check out Moqui Cave. At $5/person, it's a little pricey, especially since you'll spend less than a half hour touring the exhibits, but it's quirky, fun, and has the self-proclaimed largest fluorescent rock display in the United States. You'll also find an extensive display of Ancestral Puebloan pottery, artifacts, and arrowheads.

IN THE AREA

ACCOMMODATIONS

Cliff Dwellers Lodge, Marble Canyon. Call 928-355-2261 or 1-800-962-9755. Established as a small trading post in 1920, the lodge consists of a 20-unit motel, separate guest house for families and groups, fly shop, convenience store, restaurant, bar, and gas station. Rates start at $80/night. Web site: www.cliffdwellerslodge.com.

Grand Canyon Lodge North Rim. Call 1-877-386-4383. Located at Bright Angel Point at the North Rim of the Grand Canyon, the lodge offers cabin and motel accommodations. Cabins start at $121/night and motel rooms at $116/night. Extra charged for rim view. Web site: www.foreverlodging.com.

Jacob Lake Inn, US 89A and AZ 67, Jacob Lake. Call 928-643-7232. For nearly 100 years, this historic inn has provided lodging for North Rim sightseers and recreationalists. Choose from historic and new cabins, hotel rooms, and motel accommodations. There's an onsite bakery that serves family-favorite recipes for sweet rolls, brownies, and even some unusual treats like the lemon zucchini cookies. The dining room is open for breakfast, lunch, and dinner. Rates from $50 to $90/night. Web site: www.jacoblake.com.

Kaibab Lodge, US 89A and AZ 67, Jacob Lake. Call 928-638-2389. Open mid-May through October, the Kaibab Lodge provides cabin accommodations with shuttle service to the North Rim of the Grand Canyon. You'll find a lounge, restaurant, and gift shop here. Pets are welcome. Cabin rentals start at $85/night. Web site: www.kaibablodge.com.

Lake Powell Resort, 100 Lakeshore Drive, Page. Call 1-888-896-3829. More hotel than resort, the accommodations at Wahweap Marina are clean and comfortable. Web site: www.lakepowell.com.

Quail Park Lodge, US 89, Kanab, UT. Call 435-215-1447. This retro cool lodge has recently updated rooms and provides four classic cruiser bicycles for guests to use. Complimentary breakfast. Rooms from $90. Web site: www.quailparklodge.com.

ATTRACTIONS AND RECREATION

Best Friends Animal Sanctuary, 5001 Angel Canyon Road, Kanab, UT. Call 435-644-2001. Visit the nearly 2,000 dogs, cats, horses, and other animals from shelters and rescue groups who call the sanctuary home, at least until they're adopted. Free tours are offered four times each day. Web site: www.bestfriends.org.

Carl Hayden Visitor Center, US 89 on the west side of Glen Canyon Dam, Page. Call 928-608-6072. If you want an overview of Glen Canyon National Recreational Area, this is the place to go, even though you'll actually have to detour to get there. The visitor center has exhibits on Glen Canyon Dam, a video, and a regional relief map. You can also tour the dam for $5. Keep in mind that this is a federal power plant with strict security measures in place. That means no purses, bags, or food on the tour. Cameras are welcome. In the summer, the visitor center is open 8–6 (call for days), and from November through February, it is open daily 8:30–4:30. (Hours are Mountain Standard Time year-round.) Web site: www.nps.gov/glca/planyourvisit /visitorcenters.htm.

Frontier Movie Town and Little Hollywood Movie Museum, 297 W. Center Street, Kanab. Call 435-644-5337. Nicknamed Little Hollywood, the area surrounding Kanab set the scene for classic movies like *The Outlaw Josey Wales* and *Planet of the Apes*. It also was the backdrop for the TV series, *Gunsmoke*. The gift shop, Frontier Movie Town, sells Native American artwork, movie memorabilia, and more. The movie museum allows you to explore sets used during production and relive Hollywood history. Free. Web site: www.frontier movietown.com.

Glen Canyon National Recreational Area, Page. Call 928-608-6200. More than 1.2 million acres, the recreational area stretches from Lees Ferry in Arizona to the Orange Cliffs of Utah. Popular area activities include boating on Lake Powell, water sports, kayaking, fishing, camping, hiking, and mountain biking. Houseboats can be rented from the Lake Powell Resorts & Marinas or Antelope Point Marina. For basic information on the area, stop by the Carl Hayden Visitor Center, located just west of the Glen Canyon Dam. Web site: www.nps.gov/glca.

Grand Canyon National Park. Call 928-638-7888. Less crowded than its South Rim counterpart, the North Rim Visitor Center is open mid-May to mid-October, 8–6. Experience the canyon on scenic drives and hikes and at 10 overlooks. A fee of $25/car is charged to enter the park. Web site: www.nps.gov/grca.

Horseshoe Bend, just before Page on US 89. It's a relatively short hike to see this iconic, horseshoe-shaped bend in the Colorado River, but the sandy terrain makes the walk somewhat strenuous, especially during the summer. Free.

John Wesley Powell Memorial Museum, 6 N. Lake Powell Boulevard, Page. Call 928-645-9496. Although the museum is dedicated to John Wesley Powell and his exploration of the Colorado River, it also displays Native American and pioneer artifacts. You can also schedule river trips, boat outings, scenic flights, guided tours of Antelope Canyon, and houseboat rentals here. Web site: www.powell museum.org.

Lees Ferry, 6 miles off US 89A, Marble Canyon. Call 928-608-6200. The only place where the Colorado River could be crossed for hundreds of miles, Lees Ferry served pioneers and settlers until it was replaced by the Navajo Bridge. Today, you can tour this historic outpost, where you'll see a stone fort, ranch, and the remnants of a steamboat in the Colorado River. Web site: www.nps.gov /glca/planyourvisit/lees-ferry.htm.

Lees Ferry Anglers and Fly Shop, Marble Canyon. Call 928-355-2261 or 1-800-962-9755. Established in 1989, this full-service fly shop also provides river-boat and walk/wade guides. Web site: www.leesferry.com.

Moqui Cave, 4518 N. US 89, Kanab, Utah. Call 435-644-8525. Moqui Cave displays Ancestral Puebloan exhibits, fossils, dinosaur tracks, and the self-proclaimed largest fluorescent rock display in the United States. Open Monday through Saturday: 9–7 during the summer and 10–4 during the winter. Admission is $5/person. Web site: www.moquicave.com.

Navajo Bridge, located on US 89A. Call the Interpretive Center at 928-355-2319. Built to replace Lees Ferry, the original Navajo Bridge operated for 66 years. Although you can't drive across the original bridge, you can walk it. Open April through October, daily 9–5. Web site: www.nps.gov/glca/historyculture/navajobridge.htm.

Pipe Spring National Monument, Fredonia. Call 928-643-7105. The visitor center at Pipe Spring National Monument houses a museum with 12 exhibits focusing on the Kaibab Band of Paiute Indians and on early Mormon settlers. Guided tours of Winsor Castle—a fortified ranch house—leave every half-hour and last approximately 30 minutes. You can also take a self-guided tour that includes the East and West Cabins, garden, orchard, and corrals populated by horses and longhorn cattle. Open daily 7–5. Admission is $5/person, free for children under 16. Web site: www.nps.gov/pisp.

Vermillion Cliffs National Monument, US 89A. Call 435-688-3200. This remote area features incredible sandstone formations, rugged canyons, and backpacking opportunities. Watch for California condors, recently reintroduced to the region. Web site: www.blm.gov.

DINING

Bonkers Restaurant, 810 N. Navajo, Page. Call 928-645-2706. Entrées range from lamb, steak, and trout to Italian classics and burgers. Lunch and dinner. Web site: www.dreamkatcherslakepowell.com/bonkers_menu.html.

Cliff Dwellers Restaurant, Marble Canyon. Call 928-355-2261 or 1-800-962-9755. Located at the Cliff Dwellers Lodge, this restaurant serves fajitas, baby back ribs, lamb, fish, and more. Sandwiches are also available. Web site: www.cliffdwellerslodge.com.

Jacob Lake Inn Restaurant, US 89A and AZ 67, Jacob Lake. Call 928-643-7232. Savor made-from-scratch treats here like buttermilk pancakes; sandwiches made with freshly baked honey whole wheat or white bread; and the house specialty, Kaibab Jagerschnitzel. Open for breakfast, lunch, and dinner. Web site: www.jacoblake.com.

Kaibab Restaurant, US 89A and AZ 67, Jacob Lake. Call 928-638-2389. The restaurant at Kaibab Lodge offers a basic menu of sandwiches, pasta, chicken, salmon, and steak. Enjoy breakfast, lunch, or dinner. Web site: www.kaibablodge.com.

Rewind Diner, 18 E. Center Street, Kanab. Call 435-644-3200. Burgers, salads, soups, sandwiches, and pasta dishes dominate the menu at this diner, but you'll also find vegetarian dishes and great soda-fountain treats. Web site: www.rewinddiner.com.

Rocking V Café, 97 W. Center Street, Kanab, UT. Call 435-644-8001. The sophisticated food at Rocking V Café, like almond-crusted chicken Marsala and salmon creole, shouldn't surprise you—after all, there's an art gallery upstairs featuring local artists. Housed in Kanab's original mercantile, this restaurant serves breakfast, lunch, and dinner. Web site: www .rockingvcafe.com.

OTHER CONTACTS

Antelope Point Marina, 537 Marina Parkway, Page. Call 928-645-5900. Owned and operated by the Navajo Tribe, the marina provides houseboat rentals and guided tours through Antelope Point Outfitters. For a unique dining experience, stop by Ja'di' Tooh, the world's largest floating restaurant. Web site: www.antelopepoint lakepowell.com.

City of Page Tourism. Web site: www.pagelakepowelltourism.com.

Grand Canyon North Rim. Forever Resorts operates the lodge, restaurants, and mule rides on the North Rim. Their Web site provides information on activities and services available. Web site: www.foverever lodging.com.

Lake Powell Resorts & Marinas, Page. Call 888-896-3829. Managed by Aramark Parks and Destinations, the resort and marina offer more than a lodge, campground, and houseboat rentals. You can rent power boats and water toys, savor a dinner cruise, or take a boat tour to Rainbow Bridge. The Web site provides detailed information on what to do and see at the lake. Web site: www.lakepowell.com.

Southern Utah's Kane County, 78 S. 100 East, Kanab. Call 435-644-5033. Online information includes a calendar of events, dining and lodging information, and a listing of local attractions. Web site: www.kaneutah .com.

VisitKanab.com. Call 435-644-2534. The tourism Web site for Kanab gives viewers information on local attractions, historical sites, state and national parks, dining, lodging, and more.

Bryce Canyon National Park

11 The Indian Cultures of Scenic Southern Utah

Estimated length: 124 miles on Scenic Byway 12

Estimated time: 3 hours to Torrey

Getting there: From Salt Lake City, go south on 1-15 for 210 miles. Turn left at Exit 95 for UT 20 and drive 20 miles to US 89. Head south to UT 12. From Kanab and northern Arizona, take US 89 north 60 miles to UT 12.

Highlights: Scenic Byway 12 passes through Red Canyon, Bryce Canyon National Park, Grand Staircase-Escalante National Monument, and Capitol Reef National Park. You'll drive through some of the Southwest's most awe-inspiring country while learning about the Ancestral Puebloans, Fremont Culture, and the Southern Paiutes who inhabited the area.

Unlike most of the drives in this book, Scenic Byway 12 doesn't link one Ancestral Puebloan ruin to another or go through existing Indian Reservations. In fact, it's easy to forget that this area was once the territory of ancient hunter-gatherers and later the Paiutes. Utes, Hopi, and Shoshoni make brief appearances in the area as well, and of course Mormon settlers played a major role in the recent history of the area. Keep this in mind as you drive, and you'll gain a deeper appreciation for this beautifully rugged landscape.

Begin by turning east off US 89 onto UT 12. Within miles you enter a rocky red area that is easily confused with Bryce Canyon but is, in fact, part of the Dixie National Forest. Red Canyon features 4 miles of spires, hoodoos, turrets, and pinnacles against the backdrop of a vibrant blue sky. To the right, a 5-mile bicycle path runs alongside the highway, accessible at the first parking area. Don't miss

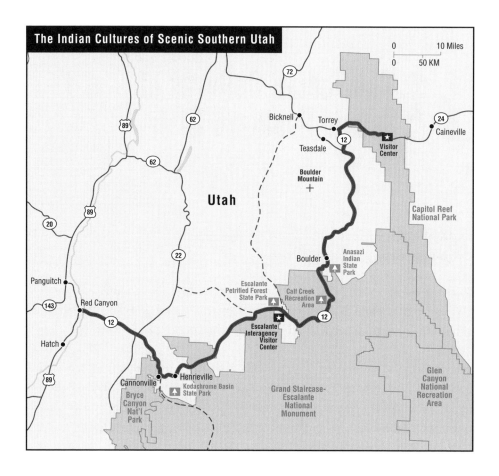

the Red Canyon Visitor Center, where you can learn about the region and available activities, like hiking, camping, riding off-highway vehicles (OHV) in designated areas, and even cross-country skiing during the winter.

The rocks soon give way to grasslands. On the right, it's hard to miss the Bryce Museum, a wildlife museum showcasing more than 800 animals recreated by Brian Wignall, whose work appears in the Smithsonian and in Bass Pro Shops. You'll also see Ancestral Puebloan artifacts on display here. Next to the museum, OHVs and bikes line the parking lot, available for rent.

Watch for UT 63, the turn for Bryce Canyon City and Bryce Canyon National Park. Turn right. Before you get to the park's entrance, you have the option to ditch your vehicle and instead take a shuttle through the park. Even though you won't be driving, you still have to pay the $25/vehicle entrance fee, so if you are short on time, skip the shuttle and drive through the park yourself. If you plan to spend the day or even stay overnight, though, the shuttle is a good option.

You can bypass the Bryce Canyon Visitor Center near the park's entrance. Although the center boasts an award-winning video, it's overrun with tourists clamoring for permits and area information. Instead, proceed to the lookouts, a 37-mile roundtrip drive (18 miles in, 18 miles out).

PRAIRIE DOG CROSSING

U tah prairie dogs, the rarest in the United States, live only in southwestern Utah, constructing underground towns where they sleep, hide and hibernate. While in Bryce Canyon, watch for roadside PRAIRIE DOG CROSSING signs.

Named after Mormon pioneer Ebenezer Bryce, the "canyon" is, ironically, not really a canyon in that erosion—not flowing water—created the unique landscape you'll see at each lookout. Freezing temperatures, wind, and rain created this geological wonder. On average, Bryce Canyon experiences 200 days a year where the temperature rises above freezing during the day and dips back below freezing at night. The ice exerts a force that pries and shatters the rocks apart, leaving the debris to be swept away by wind and rain.

While no significant ruins or evidence of Native Americans have been dis-

HOW DO HOODOOS COME TO BE?

T wo weathering processes created the totem pole–shaped rock formations in Bryce Canyon National Park. In the winter, water from melting snow seeps into the cracks of the Paunsaugunt Plateau and freezes at night, expanding by 10 percent. Bit by bit, it pries open the cracks in a process called frost wedging.

Wind and rain then washes the debris away and further erodes the layers. Eventually a hole or window pokes through the rocky arm and finally, the piece separates to become its own formation, a hoodoo. Unfortunately, this erosion process continues, wearing down the hoodoo to nothing.

WHO WERE THE INDIANS OF THE FREMONT CULTURE?

The Indians of the Fremont Culture take their name from the Fremont River, where the remnants of their culture were first discovered. Little is known for sure about them, but since they are similar in many ways to the Ancestral Puebloans, it's theorized that perhaps they split off from the main group or that they emerged from the same archaic desert culture as the Ancestral Puebloans.

Although the Fremont and Ancestral Puebloan cultures are strikingly similar, four distinct characteristics separate them:

❖ The use of a one-rod-and-bundle method to weave baskets

❖ Moccasins constructed from a deer or sheep, instead of woven yucca

❖ Rock art featuring trapezoidal human figures with blunt hairstyles

❖ Thin gray pottery with smooth, polished surfaces

It's unclear what happened to the Fremont Culture, but they seem to have disappeared between 1250 and 1500 A.D., either due to climate change or displacement.

covered within Bryce Canyon, the Fremont Culture and Ancestral Puebloans occupied this region from approximately 200 to 1200 A.D. Later, the Paiutes frequented the area to harvest pine nuts and hunt for rabbits. According to Paiute legend, Coyote turned their ancestors, the Legend People, into rocks in Bryce Canyon, and you can see them today in the park's hoodoos and formations.

After leaving the park, return to UT 12 and turn right. The landscape changes from red rocks to fertile farmland as you approach Tropic, and you begin to skirt the edge of the **Grand Staircase-Escalante National Monument**. Utah's newest national monument encompasses nearly 1.9 million acres with three distinct sections: the Grand Staircase, the Kaiparowits Plateau, and the Canyons of the Escalante. Turn right on Main Street in Cannonville, and drive a few hundred feet to one of the Grand Staircase-Escalante visitor centers.

Each of the five visitor centers within the national monument's boundary focuses on a particular theme—paleontology in Big Water; archaeology and geology in Kanab; ecology and biology in Escalante; the Ancestral Puebloans in Boulder; and human geography in Cannonville. Displays of artifacts, murals, and oral histories at the Cannonville Visitor Center depict what life was like for the Paiute and the pioneers. The center also has a topographic relief model of the national monument and an ethnobotanical garden.

If you continue south on Main Street, you'll come to Kodachrome Basin State Park, named by the National Geographic Society after the popular color film. The park boasts 67 towering spires and several hiking trails. Ten miles southeast of Kodachrome, you can also view Grosvenor Arch, an intricate double arch. Unpaved roads through the area lead to backcountry points within Grand Staircase-Escalante National Monument.

From Cannonville, continue through Henrieville toward Escalante. Along the way, prepare to pull over at the Upper Blues Overlook and the Upper Valley Granaries Pullout. The first stop overlooks the green-gray mudstone and sandstone

Grand Staircase-Escalante National Monument covers 1.9 million acres in Southern Utah.

known as The Blues, a fossil-rich area dating to the late Cretaceous Period. Less than 10 miles down the road, stop at the Upper Valley Granaries Pullout and peer through the viewing tube to locate the small structure used by the Fremont Culture as a storage place for grain and other food.

The town of Escalante is often referred to as "the Heart of Scenic Byway 12," and it serves as the mid-point of the journey. Reserve at least an hour to thoroughly explore the area, beginning with the Escalante Petrified Forest State Park, adjacent to Wide Hollow Reservoir. Hike through a 160-million-year-old petrified forest, fish the reservoir, or rent a canoe. The park also has a visitor center that displays petrified wood and fossilized dinosaur bones. Then, head to the Escalante Interagency Visitor Center, located a mile past the turnoff for the petrified forest, on the right side of UT 12. The center houses ecology and biology displays, including murals, photographs, and dioramas. Information on visiting the local area and the Grand Staircase-Escalante National Monument is also available.

Get ready for another series of scenic overlooks as you leave Escalante. Head of the Rocks Overlook is the first, just 10 miles outside of town. As you look out over the cream sandstone formations, you can see Boulder Mountain to the north, the Little Rockies and Henry Mountains to the east, and Navajo Mountain to the southwest. Below, the byway snakes through the rocks. Grab your camera. It makes for an incredible photo.

Boyton Overlook showcases the flowing waters of the Escalante River and its riparian area. Although you can't see it from above, ruins and rock art can be found here, evidence of ancient civilizations.

A short but twisty 2 miles later, you enter the Calf Creek Recreation Area. The beautiful box canyon takes its name from the early settlers' practice of bringing newly weaned calves to these natural pasturelands to separate them from their mothers. Gone are the cows but, aside from the highway, this tranquil oasis remains roughly unchanged. Two waterfalls make the area a favorite with hikers. While the Upper Falls can only be reached by a strenuous hike over slickrock formations, the 126-foot-high Lower Calf Creek Falls is more accessible—a 5.5-mile roundtrip trek through sand, but with relatively little elevation change. Along the way, watch for pictographs.

The stretch of UT 12 known as The Hogsback hugs a thin strip of slickrock just north of Calf Creek. On either side, the steep ridge drops into caynonlands just feet from your passenger side tires. You definitely want to drive the speed limit and stay focused. Think freeway overpass without the concrete guardrails.

It only takes a few minutes to get from The Hogsback to Boulder. Located at the base of Boulder Mountain, the small community is so remote that, until 1935, mail was delivered by horse and fresh milk often turned to butter on the rough roads from Escalante. Present-day Boulder boasts two lodges and dining options that feature fresh local produce. But Boulder is best known for the Anasazi State Park Museum. The 6-acre consists of a museum displaying ancient artifacts from the area and the Coombs site, one of the largest Ancestral Puebloan communities found west of the Colorado River. Believed to have been occupied between 1160 and 1235 A.D., the village may have housed up to 200 people.

The scenery along the way to Capitol Reef National Park

Soon after leaving Boulder, you begin to climb the mountain that shares its name. Boulder Mountain is part of the Dixie National Forest and rises 11,000 feet above Capitol Reef National Park. From Homestead Overlook, you can see parts of Capitol Reef, and to the south you can see all the way to Navajo Mountain on a clear day. Aspens cover the mountain, making the drive particularly spectacular during the fall when the trees' leaves change to brilliant orange, yellow, and red.

Descending from Boulder Mountain, you enter Torrey, where UT 12 dead-ends into UT 24. The small town, named for Colonel Jay Torrey, one of Theodore Roosevelt's Rough Riders, has a few chain hotels and not much else. Although the drive is technically over here, you can't leave the area without first visiting Capitol Reef National Park, a 10-mile detour. Turn right on UT 24.

A giant buckle in the Earth's crust formed the colorful jumble of cliffs, domes, spires, monoliths, arches, and canyons of Capitol Reef. Stretching for nearly 100 miles, the 65-million-year-old geographical landform is technically a monocline, a regional fold or step-up in the rock layers. Early explorers mistakenly labeled what is known, geographically, as the Waterpocket Fold a *reef*. The moniker *capitol* comes from the white domes of Navajo sandstone that resemble capitol building domes.

Take your time driving to the park. From Torrey to the visitor center, the drive has several pullouts along UT 24 where you can photograph formations like Chimney Rock and The Castle; or take in the Waterpocket Fold from a distance at Goosenecks Overlook. Drive carefully, since people dart in and out of these pullouts.

Before you actually turn into the park, continue the short distance to Fruita Schoolhouse, less than a mile farther on the left. Originally, a flat, dirt roof covered the school made of bare, chinked logs. Later, settlers added a peaked, shingle roof and plastered the interior of the turn-of-the-century building. Homemade pine desks lined the classroom, where teachers instructed through the eighth grade until the school closed in 1941, due to a lack of students.

Just past the school, pull over to view the Fremont Culture petroglyphs. The impressive rock art shows large figures with headdresses surrounded by smaller animal figures. Viewing tubes are available, but you shouldn't need them. The pictures are carved into the base of the sandstone.

Capitol Reef National Park includes a historic Mormon settlement and orchards.

Return to the park entrance. On your right is the visitor center. Although it's mainly a gift shop, you may want to stop inside and find out what fruit can be picked from the park's historic orchards. The park service Web site lists approximate flowering and harvesting times, but depending on the weather, these dates could be off. If you want to see a particular blossom or pick a specific fruit, call ahead (there's an option for the fruit hotline on the park's main phone number). Otherwise, stop at the visitor center to see what the orchards have to offer.

The orchards at Capitol Reef National Park

Deer graze in the fields of Capitol Reef National Park.

The orchards, planted during the 1880s by the Mormon pioneers, contain approximately 2,700 trees, including apple, pear, peach, cherry, apricot, mulberry, plum, walnut, and almond. You are welcome to enter any unlocked orchard and consume as much fruit as you want while there. Pickers and ladders are available for your use. However, if you want to take any home with you, you'll be asked to pick your fruit, weigh it at the weigh station, and pay what you owe (usually $1/pound). Payment is usually on the honor system.

From the visitor center, continue right into the park. You'll see the tree-lined Fremont River to your left. When you come to the blacksmith's shop, park and walk across the street to the Ripple Rock Nature Center. The center has interactive displays and exhibits and maintains a schedule of activities. Spend some time exploring the property, especially the Fremont River, which runs directly behind the small, red building.

Around the bend, Gifford Farm serves as an example of Fruita life in the early 1900s. The site consists of the farmhouse, barn, smokehouse, garden, and pasture. You can tour the home's museum. A gift shop there sells reproduction utensils, household items from era, jams, jellies, dried fruit, homemade ice cream, and locally baked pies.

Past the farm and its neighboring campground, a pay station collects the $5/vehicle fee for access to the scenic drive. Before you continue, read the postings for notice of any closed backroads or trails. Although the main road is paved, the backroads are not and, as a result, are subject to flooding. Note, too, the vehicle restrictions; tight turns necessitate limiting vehicles' length.

If you're interested, the visitor center sells guides for the scenic drive, which skirts along the edge of the Waterpocket Fold. Park service brochures recommend two hours for the one-way, 10-mile trip, but depending on what you want to do and exactly how far you go, you could budget half of that.

When you finish visiting Capitol Reef, you have several options. You can head north to Salt Lake City, a 3.5-hour drive taking UT 24 to UT 260, US 50, and I-15. Or you can take UT 24 to UT 62 and then US 89, again a 3.5-hour drive. But for a truly spectacular drive, head east on UT 24 to Hanksville and take UT 95 to Lake Powell, through Fry Canyon and past Natural Bridges National Monument. Soon after the monument, turn right on UT 261 and continue to Moki Dugway, a 5-mile-per-hour dirt road built in 1958 to transport uranium ore from the Happy Jack mine in Fry Canyon to the processing mill in Mexican Hat. Because the route consists of sharp switchbacks, it is not recommended for RVs.

Petroglyphs in Capitol Reef National Park

IN THE AREA

ACCOMMODATIONS

Austin's Chuckwagon Lodge and General Store, 12 W. Main Street, Torrey. Call 1-800-863-3288. The lodge offers motel rooms and cabins with two bedrooms, living room, kitchen, and bathroom. An onsite general store also includes a deli and bakery. Standard rooms start at $75/night, cabins at $135/night, and a family suite at $150/night. Web site: www .austinschuckwagonmotel.com.

Boulder Mountain Guest Ranch, 3621 Hells Backbone Road, Boulder. Call 435-335-7480. The ranch has three cabins and a main lodge with six rooms. Lodge rooms are $70/night; cabins begin at $95/night and include a private deck and fire pit. Web site: www.bouldermountainguestranch .com.

Boulder Mountain Lodge, 20 N. UT 12, Boulder. Call 435-335-7460. This luxury lodge sports massive timbers and rusted metal roofs. Rates depend on the season with rooms starting at $79/night during the winter months of December, January, and February. High-season rates start at $130/night and go up to $200/night for the two-bedroom unit. The lodge restaurant, Hell's Backbone Grill, serves American and Southwestern fare. Web site: www.boulder-utah.com.

Ruby's Inn, 26. S. Main, Bryce Canyon City. Call 435-834-5341 or 1-866-866-6616. Originated by Reuben C. (Ruby) Syrett, the hotel offers the closest accommodations to Bryce Canyon National Park and easy access to the shuttle. Campsites and RV spots are also available. Rates from $72/night. Web site: www.rubysinn.com.

Slot Canyons Inn Bed & Breakfast, 3680 W. UT 12, Escalante. Call 435-826-4901 or 1-866-889-8375. The bed & breakfast, which has eight rooms for rent and a 1,600-square foot cabin, sits directly in front of an excavation site that dates back 11,000 years, making it the oldest site on the northern Colorado Plateau. Rates from $159/night. Web site: www.slot canyonsinn.com.

ATTRACTIONS AND RECREATION

Anasazi State Park Museum, 460 N. UT 12, Boulder. Call 435-335-7308. Visit one of the largest Ancestral Puebloan communities found west of the Colorado River, with its more than 100 structures. The museum also houses many of the thousands of artifacts discovered in the area. Open April through October, daily 8–6; November through March, Monday through Saturday, 9–5. Admission is $5/person, $3/senior, or $10/family.

Bryce Canyon National Park, UT 63, Bryce Canyon City. Call 435-834-5322. Not really a canyon, the 52.6-mile national park features brilliantly colored hoodoos created by rain and by water freezing, thawing, and freezing again in the rocks' cracks. Visitors are encouraged to use the free shuttle service, but you can also drive yourself to the overlooks. Hiking, camping, and horseback riding are permitted within the park. The entrance fee is $25/vehicle. Web site: www.nps.gov/brca.

Bryce Museum, 1945 W. UT 12, Bryce. Call 435-834-5555. This natural history museum showcases 800 animals in accurate wildlife habitat murals, plus a collection of seashells, Ancestral Puebloan artifacts, animal skulls, and 1,600 butterflies. You can also feed the museum's deer. Off-highway vehicles and bikes are available for rent, too. The museum is open April 1 through November 15, daily 9–7. Admission is $8/person. Web site: www.brycewildlifeadventure.com.

Calf Creek Recreation Area, UT 12. This box canyon is known for its waterfalls and streaked sandstone cliffs. Camping, hiking, and picnicking are available. No fee to visit; $5/night to camp, on a first-come basis.

Cannonville Visitor Center, 10 Center Street, Cannonville. Call 435-826-5640. The center displays exhibits on the human geography of the Grand Staircase-Escalante National Monument and surrounding area. Open mid-March to mid-November, daily 8–4:30. Free.

Capitol Reef National Park, Torrey. Call 435-425-3791. (For information on what fruit is available to be picked, listen for the Fruit Hotline option.) This Mormon pioneer settlement has historic buildings, like the Gifford Farm and Fruita Schoolhouse, plus orchards where you can pick ripe fruit and eat it in the park. Or, for $1/pound, you can take what you pick home. Open daily 8–4:30, with extended hours during the summer. There's no fee to drive to Fruitopa, but if you want to explore the scenic drive, there's a charge of $3/person or $5/vehicle. Web site: www.nps.gov/care.

Escalante Interagency Visitor Center, 755 W. UT 12, Escalante. Call 435-826-5499. The center displays exhibits on the ecology and biology of the Grand Staircase-Escalante National Monument and surrounding area. Open daily 8–4:30. Free.

Escalante Petrified Forest State Park, 710 N. Resevoir Road, Escalante. Call 435-826-4466. Located 1 mile west of UT 12, the state park visitor center displays petrified wood and fossilized dinosaur bones over 100 million years old. You can hike the nature trails or enjoy adjacent Wide Hollow Reservoir. Open daily: 7 AM–10 PM during the summer, 8 AM–10 PM during the winter. Day use fee of $6/vehicle is charged. Web site: www.stateparks.utah.gov/parks/escalante.

Scenic Byway 12 cuts through Southern Utah.

Grand Staircase-Escalante National Monument. Call 435-644-4300. The 1.9-million acres of Utah's newest national monument connects Glen Canyon National Recreation Area with Capitol Reef and Bryce Canyon National Parks and features multicolored cliffs, natural bridges, sandstone arches, mesas, buttes, and the Escalante River. In addition to hiking, mountain biking, and camping, you can climb the steep cliffs here, navigate the river, horseback ride, hunt, fish, and even use your off-highway vehicle (OHV) in designated areas. There is no fee to enter, although free permits—available at the monument's five visitor centers—are required for some activities. Web site: www.blm.gov/ut/st/en/fo/grand _staircase-escalante.html.

Kodachrome Basin State Park, Cannonville. Call 435-679-8562. Named after the popular color film, the park offers spectacular views of monolith spires and red rock formations. Open daily 6 AM–10 PM. A day use fee of $6/vehicle is charged. Web site: www.stateparks.utah.gov/parks /kodachrome.

Red Canyon. Call 435-865-3700. The vermillion-colored rock formations and Ponderosa pines of this canyon are part of the Dixie National Forest. An extensive trail system and road-side bike trail make touring the area a breeze. Free. Web site: www.fs.usda.gov.

DINING

Burr Trail Grill, 10 N. US 12, Boulder. Call 435-335-7503. Open seasonally for breakfast, lunch, and dinner, the restaurant features local products, including local beef. Wine and beer are available. Web site: www.burrtrail grill.com.

Café Diablo, 599 UT 24, Torrey. Call 435-425-3070. Owner and chef, Gary Pankow, a graduate of the Culinary Institute of America, serves upscale cuisine like Utah lamb, pumpkin seed trout, and crown rack of glazed ribs. Save room for the homemade ice cream and the pastry team's creations. Web site: www.cafediablo.net.

The Rim Rock, 2523 UT 24, Torrey. Call 435-425-3388. You can sit on the patio for a casual dining experience or dine in the restaurant for a more upscale meal. Each option comes with a separate menu. The patio dishes up Italian foods like pasta and pizza as well as Western favorites like barbecue while the restaurant focuses on fresh, local cuisine like seared trout and hand-cut steaks. Web site: www.therimrock.net.

Slackers, 165 E. UT 24, Torrey. Call 435-425-3710. Enjoy the great hamburgers and sweet potato fries. The restaurant also has salads, chicken, and more.

OTHER CONTACTS

Bryce Canyon Country.com, Garfield County Office of Tourism. Call 435-676-1161 or 1-800-444-6689. This travel-planning Web site has helpful video shorts and offers a free Bryce Canyon Country smart phone app. Web site: www.brycecanyoncountry.com.

Dixie National Forest. Call 435-865-3719. Many of the sites along the way are part of the Dixie National Forest, like Red Canyon and Boulder Mountain. Call or go online for additional information. Web site: www.fs.usda.gov.

Escalante Chamber of Commerce, Escalante. The chamber provides information on local communities, accommodations, restaurants, shops, and activities. Web site: www.escalante-cc.com.

Scenic Byway 12.com. The online resource offers detailed information about the byway's sites. Check out the map—it's particularly useful. Web site: www.scenicbyway12.com.

The Sky Walk at Grand Canyon West

12 The Tribe at the West Rim

Estimated length: 128 miles to Grand Canyon West

Estimated time: 3 to 4 hours, depending on road conditions

Getting there: From I-40, take Exit 123 into Seligman.

Highlights: Travel historic Route 66 through Seligman toward Kingman, visiting quirky attractions, shops, and eateries along the way. In Peach Springs, you can book a Colorado River rafting trip or detour to Havasupai. A scenic drive through a Joshua tree forest brings you to Grand Canyon West, the overlook owned and operated by the Hualapai Nation. There, helicopter over the canyon. Or, walk over it. The tribe operates the Skywalk, a glass bridge suspended 4,000 feet above the Colorado River below.

Several routes cut through the Hualapai Indian Reservations toward Grand Canyon West. Tourists from Las Vegas go south through Boulder on US 93. Visitors from California usually drive across on I-40 to Kingman and head north on US 93. Both turn on Pierce Ferry Road and continue to the site, and if all you're interested in is seeing the Grand Canyon, these are the quickest routes to take. However, if you want to experience Route 66 and Hualapai culture, start from Seligman.

To pick up Route 66, take I-40 Exit 123. One of the nation's first highways, The Mother Road officially began service in November 1926 as a roadway that connected Chicago to Los Angeles, running through the states of Illinois, Missouri, Kansas, Oklahoma, Texas, New Mexico, Arizona, and California. In 1985, the United States Department of Transportation decommissioned Route 66, and

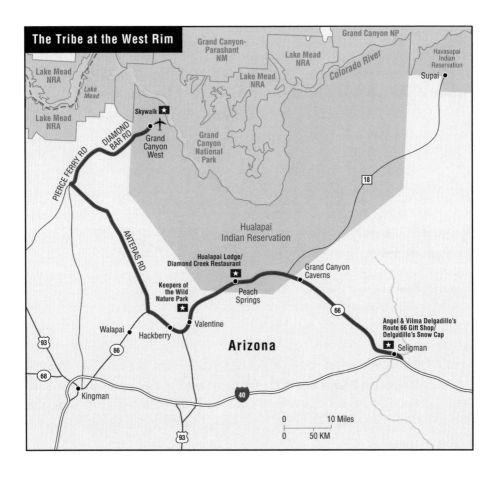

The Tribe at the West Rim

Grand Canyon NP

Grand Canyon-Parashant NM

Lake Mead NRA

Colorado River

Havasupai Indian Reservation

Lake Mead NRA

Lake Mead NRA

Lake Mead

Lake Mead NRA

Supai •

Skywalk ★

Grand Canyon West

Grand Canyon National Park

18

Hualapai Indian Reservation

PIERCE FERRY RD

DIAMOND BAR RD

ANTERAS RD

Hualapai Lodge/ Diamond Creek Restaurant ★

Keepers of the Wild Nature Park ★

Peach Springs

Grand Canyon Caverns

Walapai •

Hackberry •

Valentine •

93

66

Arizona

66

Angel & Vilma Delgadillo's Route 66 Gift Shop/ Delgadillo's Snow Cap ★ Seligman

68

Kingman

40

0   10 Miles

0   50 KM

93

the road's signs came down. Angel Delgadillo, the Seligman barber, watched as his town began to slowly die.

But Angel was not about to go down without a fight. While others tried to lure industry into the community, he realized that the route had nostalgic potential, so he helped form the Historic Route 66 Association of Arizona. In 1987, he also successfully lobbied the Arizona Legislature to designate Route 66 as a historic highway. Following Arizona's lead, the seven other states along the historic highway also formed associations, and the road that once got people to their destinations now is a destination itself.

You can still visit The Guardian Angel of Route 66 at his Seligman barbershop, which since his retirement has evolved into a gift store and visitor center. At **Angel & Vilma Delgadillo's Route 66 Gift Shop**, you can shop for Route 66 memorabilia, flip through albums of photos sent to Angel by visitors, or add a business card to the thousands already tacked on the walls. Although in his 80s, Angel will still pose for photos and share stories about the town and highway he loves.

As you enter Seligman, watch for Delgadillo's Snow Cap. The drive-in is hard to miss: ice-cream cones top the white building adorned with reddish-orange highlights. Bright chairs sit under the patio on one side; on the other, you'll find a 1936 Chevrolet adorned with flowers and an artificial Christmas tree. Opened by Angel's brother, Juan, in 1953, the drive-in is known for its sense of humor as much as it is for its food. Need a straw? You'll receive a clump of the barnyard variety. Want ice cream? Expect a cup of ice with cream on top. It doesn't matter what you order or ask for, the Delgadillos go for the laugh. Sadly, Juan passed away in 2004. His children and grandchildren now run the drive-in.

Before you leave Seligman, fill up your gas tank. Stations at Grand Canyon

When in Seligman, stop by Delgadillo's Snow Cap for a burger and a good time.

Caverns and Truxton tend to be higher priced and close for the night, so if you get desperate, you might have to drive all the way to Kingman to refuel. Whatever you do, though, don't head out on Antares Road without enough gas to get to the Grand Canyon West and back to Kingman, approximately 140 miles. There are no gas stations at the canyon.

Route 66 retraces the government-funded wagon road built by U.S. Army surveyor Lieutenant Edward Fitzgerald Beale in the 1850s, and for the most part, it runs parallel to the Burlington Northern and Santa Fe Railway. As you head toward Peach Springs, watch for the sequentially spaced Burma Shave signs on your right. The signs feature snappy sayings like IF DAISIES ARE YOUR FAVORITE FLOWER, KEEP PUSHING UP THOSE MILES PER HOUR, and are reminiscent of World War II–era America.

At Milemarker 115, Grand Canyon Caverns appears on your left. Railroad woodcutter Walter Peck discovered the caverns after nearly falling into a large, funnel-shaped hole while on his way to play poker in 1927. The next day, he explored the hole and found two skeletons, a saddle, and what he thought was gold. Peck purchased the property, intending to mine it, only to learn later that his "gold" was actually iron oxide or in other words rust. In the meantime, newspapers picked up on the story and reported that Peck had discovered "cavemen" in his cavern.

Determined to make the best of his situation, he started charging visitors a quarter to see where he found the cavemen. The curious—Peck called them "dopes on a rope"—had to provide their own light source. They were then tied to the end of a rope and lowered 210 feet, the equivalent of 21 stories, into the darkness.

The experience today is quite different. An elevator brings you to the cavern floor with its well-lit concrete paths, and you have three tours to choose from: a 25-minute, a 45-minute, and an explorer's tour. During your visit, you'll see flowstone rock formations and walls glittering with selenite crystals. On property, horseback rides at Quarter Circle JD or jeep tours to the bottom of the Grand Canyon can be arranged.

A few miles past the caverns, you enter the Hualapai Reservation. Hunter-gatherers, the People of the Tall Pines once inhabited nearly 5 million acres; the present-day reservation occupies only one-fifth of that area, including 108 miles of the Colorado River and Grand Canyon. It also extends to Peach Springs, where

A coyote on the way to the Grand Canyon West.

the tribe operates the 60-room **Hualapai Lodge**. The adjoining **Diamond Creek Restaurant** dishes up pork chile verde, Native American stew, and Hualapai tacos, in addition to burgers and sandwiches.

Continuing west, you pass through the small communities of Truxton and Valentine. Watch for a 1956 Chevy, a 76 gas station overgrown with weeds, and several vintage pick-up trucks, all reminders of a bygone era. You'll also spot **Keepers of the Wild Nature Park**, a 175-acre animal sanctuary that serves as home to nearly 200 rescued animals, including lions, tigers, leopards, monkeys, and cougars. The price of admission allows you to walk through sanctuary and admire the animals, but for an additional $10, you can also take a guided safari tour and view predator feeding times.

Hackberry marks the end of the easy part of the drive. Look for the Kozy Corner Trailer Park on the corner of Route 66 and Anteras Road. Turn right. Although

The route to Grand Canyon West is well-marked.

it is paved for the first mile, Anteras becomes a 30-mile dirt road that is slow going for the first 10 miles but gradually becomes smoother.

Whether it takes you three hours to get from Hackberry to Grand Canyon West depends on how fast you feel comfortable driving. If you pace a steady 25 miles per hour, it could easily take three hours; if you feel comfortable accelerating to 50 miles per hour, something that is feasible to do on the flat and relatively smooth sections of road, you could shave an hour or more off your windshield time. I completed the drive in a Dodge Charger in well under 2 hours.

Near the end of Anteras Road, Joshua trees appear and eventually dominate the landscape. When you come to the stop sign, turn right onto Pierce Ferry Road and continue to Diamond Bar Road. Turn right again. The next 25 miles are another dirt road. This time, because of the sharp turns, you'll be limited to 15 to 25 miles per hour. Keep an eye out for jackrabbits, coyotes, and other wildlife as you wind toward the Grand Canyon.

Helicopters are the first sign that you've reached your destination. At any given time, expect to see at least half a dozen making the wide, sweeping loop from the airport, over the canyon, and back. You'll be directed to turn into the airport, park at the gravel parking lot, and walk to the white, tentlike structure that serves as the visitor center. Once inside, purchase tickets at the reservation counter in the gift shop.

The tickets are not cheap. By comparison, visiting the South Rim of the Grand Canyon will set you back $25/vehicle or $6.25/person for a family of four. A trip to Grand Canyon West, on the other hand, will cost $43/person just to see the canyon from two overlooks. If you want to peer down into the canyon from the Skywalk, it will cost an additional $30/person, for a total cost of $73/person. That's nearly $300 for a family of four. Other packages are available that include helicopter rides, day rafting trips, and overnight stays at Hualapai Ranch, but these options will be even more expensive.

Is it worth it? That depends. If you just want to see the Grand Canyon, go to the South Rim—it's cheaper, you're admission is good for seven days, and there's more to see and do there, like hiking into the canyon, renting bikes to ride along the rim, and touring the visitor centers and museums. But, if you want the thrill of standing over the edge of the canyon and are willing to pay nearly $75 to do it, do not miss this opportunity.

After purchasing tickets, you'll be directed through the terminal next door to the bus and shuttle boarding area. Pick a seat on the right side of the bus (near the entrance, not behind the driver), and you'll get a good view of the canyon on your way to Eagle's Point, your first stop. The buses run every 15 minutes, taking you from the first viewpoint to Guano Point and back to the boarding area. Spend as much or little time at each stop as you like.

To experience the Skywalk, enter the portable building near the food vendors. You'll be instructed to place all belongings in one of the free lockers, proceed through the security checkpoint, and take the ramp to what will one day be a visitor center, museum, gift shop, and restaurant. For now, it's nothing but exposed beams and black plastic walls inside. Slip on the booties and step out to the horseshoe-shaped glass bridge.

If you are afraid of heights, you may want to think twice before purchasing a Skywalk ticket. Even though the glass is frosted white along both sides of the walkway, it's nearly impossible to stay on the edges. Photographers crowd the

HOW DID THEY BUILD THE SKYWALK?

The highest man-made structure in the world sits 4,000 feet above the Colorado River and consists of more than 1 million pounds of steel and 83,000 pounds of glass. It can support 71 million pounds—that's 71 fully loaded 747 airplanes—and can withstand winds of up to 90 miles per hour. So, how did it come to be?

After a helicopter ride over the Grand Canyon in 1996, Las Vegas businessman David Jin had an idea—what if visitors could enjoy a similar experience by stepping out on a glass bridge that overlooked the rim? He finally won approval from the Hualapai Tribe in 2003, and after the tribe blessed the site, construction began in late 2004. Engineers drilled 46 feet into the limestone to secure the structure and then poured a foundation consisting of eight columns that support box beams.

The actual bridge was constructed onsite by welding 40-foot girders into a horseshoe shape and then rolling the massive bridge into place, employing the same rod and plate method Egyptians used in the construction of the pyramids. It took two days to settle the $31-million bridge into its final position. The Skywalk opened to the general public on March 28, 2007.

Skywalk, posing visitors and snapping pictures that can be purchased at the gift shop on the way out. Try as you may, you will at some point have to step into the clear middle space to dodge an impromptu photo session. But the experience is worth a little anxiety. Keep in mind: the bridge can hold up to 71 million pounds—the equivalent of 71 fully loaded 747 airplanes—and can withstand an earthquake of 8.0 magnitude 50 miles away.

Following your Skywalk adventure, head to the amphitheater where Native American musicians and dancers perform daily. Or take a self-guided tour of the Native American dwellings on display, beginning with a Hualapai wickiup and ending with a brick Hopi structure. Not only is it interesting to see these structures side by side, but you can also enter and get a sense of what it must have been like to live in them. When you've finished, board the bus and head for Guano Point.

A fisherman discovered guano, the Spanish word for bat excrement, in a cave near this point in the 1930s. For years, he tried to get the funding to mine the

Native American dwellings on display at Grand Canyon West

An example of a plains Indian's teepee at Grand Canyon West

HAVASUPAI AND ITS WATERFALLS

The Hualapai Tribe isn't the only tribe at the western end of the Grand Canyon—the Havasupai Indians have lived on the canyon floor, in the village of Supai, for at least 800 years. You can visit Supai, but the journey isn't an easy one.

From Peach Springs, head east on Route 66 and turn left at Indian Route 19/Nelson Road. Since you can expect the 70-mile drive to Hualapai Hilltop to take approximately three hours and the hike down into the canyon is 8 miles, you'll definitely want to reserve a campsite before you go, especially since visitors who show up without a reservation are charged double the rate. (The entrance fee is $35/person, plus a $5/person environmental fee. The campground fee is $17/person per night, for an overnight total of $57.)

The hike into the canyon starts off steep and with switchbacks for 1.5 miles. It is considered moderately difficult. You can arrange to ride a horse or mule to the campground ($187 roundtrip) or carry your gear to the bottom for you. Helicopters can also take you in and out of the canyon ($85/person, each way).

For most visitors, the allure isn't the village with its small café, lodge, general store, and public buildings. It's not even the post office, the only post office in the United States where mail is delivered by pack train. It's the blue-green waterfalls located beyond the village. Major changes have occurred since the 2008 flashfloods swept through here, including the addition of two new falls, but the bright waters against the reddish rock are still a spectacular sight.

It's no wonder the Havasupai are known as the *Havsuw'Baaja* or Blue Water People. For more information, contact the tribe at 928-448-2121 or visit their Web site: www.havasupaitribe.com.

guano, a key component in fertilizer, explosives, pharmaceuticals, and makeup, but finally, he gave up and sold the property to the U.S. Guano Corporation in 1957. Using hoses, they sucked the guano out of the cave near the floor and loaded it into an aerial tram to be removed from the canyon. Mining ceased in early 1960 when the price of guano made it no longer a profitable venture.

An example of a Hopi dwelling's interior

Portions of the cableway remain at the point, and if you look below, you can still see the yellow car sent flying over the rim during the filming of the 1959 movie *Edge of Eternity*. Several scenes were filmed at Guano Point, including a fight sequence on the aerial tram miner's bucket, a mile above the Colorado River. If you're lucky, one of the drivers might be showing the movie on his bus. Otherwise, you'll have to try to rent or download it when you get home.

You are so secluded at this point that you don't have the option of linking up with another drive. If you want to explore the area more, head back toward Peach Springs and set out for Havasupai. Otherwise, follow the signs to Kingman and I-40.

IN THE AREA

ACCOMMODATIONS

Grand Canyon Caverns Inn, Route 66. Call 928-422-3223. The inn is a 60s-era motel that offers no frills, but for the adventurous, there's the option to stay in the Cavern Suite, a room 200 feet wide, 400 feet long, and 220 feet underground. Web site: www.gc caverns.com.

Grand Canyon Ranch, 3750 Diamond Bar Ranch Road, Meadview. Call 1-866-599-6674. Located on the dirt road 14 miles before Grand Canyon West, this ranch gives guests the option to stay in a pine cabin or tipi. Horseback riding and helicopter rides over the canyon are available for an additional charge. Room rates start at $199/night.

Hualapai Lodge, Route 66, Peach Springs. Call 928-769-2637. The 60-room lodge features Hualapai artwork, a fitness center, and a heated salt-water pool. Whether you are a guest or not, you can also arrange for

The Grand Canyon as seen from Guano Point

What remains of the cableway at Guano Point

a whitewater rafting trip through Hualapai River Runners or purchase Skywalk tickets from the concierge. Rooms from $70/night. Web site: www.grandcanyonwest.com/lodge.php.

Hualapai Ranch, Grand Canyon West, Hualapai Reservation. Stay overnight in a cabin that faces the canyon rim. Included in the $130/person rate is continental breakfast, a meal at the ranch, and the entrance fee to Grand Canyon West. Horseback rides to the rim are available for an additional charge. Web site: www.grandcanyon west.com/ranch.php.

ATTRACTIONS AND RECREATION

Angel & Vilma Delgadillo's Route 66 Gift Shop, 217 E. Route 66, Seligman. Call 928-422-3352. This combination of gift shop, visitors center, and barbershop is owned by the man credited with saving Route 66, Angel Delgadillo. Web site: www.route66gift shop.com.

Grand Canyon Caverns, Route 66. Call 928-422-4565. Descend 210 feet by elevator to tour the largest dry cavern—one that's no longer living and growing—in the United States. Open daily 9–5. The standard tour lasts 45 minutes and costs $14.95/ adult and $9.95/children ages 5–12. For those short on time, a 25-minute, wheelchair accessible tour is available. The more adventurous have the option of an explorers' tour that takes visitors off the paved trail. At least 72 hours' notice is required. Also onsite are a restaurant, adjoining curio shop, inn, and RV campground. Web site: www.gccaverns.com.

Grand Canyon West, Hualapai Reservation. Call 928-769-2636. Privately owned and operated by the Hualapai Tribe, Grand Canyon West includes Hualapai Ranch, an airport, two canyon overlooks, and the Skywalk. The entrance fee of $43/person includes shuttle service, views of the canyon from two points, a walking tour of Native American dwellings, and live cultural performances. Additional packages and add-on options, like helicopter tours, are available. The Skywalk is *not* included in general admission. Web site: www.grand canyonwest.com.

Keepers of the Wild Nature Park, 13441 E. Route 66, Valentine. Call 928-769-1800. A nonprofit organization, Keepers of the Wild protects abused, neglected, abandoned, and retired captive wildlife. If you visit, you'll see more than 175 rescued animals, including lions, tigers, leopards, monkeys, and cougars. The park is open Wednesday through Monday, 9–5. The fee is $18/adult, $15/seniors, and $12/children 12 and under. Guided safari tours are available for an additional $10/person. Web site: www.keepersofthewild.org.

A Native American dwelling at Grand Canyon West

Skywalk, Grand Canyon West, Huala-pai Reservation. Call 702-220-8372. Step out over the edge of the Grand Canyon and look down 4,000 feet as you make your way along the horse-shoe-shaped glass bridge that is the highest manmade structure in the world. You will have to purchase a $30 ticket for the experience in addition to the $43 entrance fee into Grand Canyon West, for a total of $73. No personal items, including cameras, are allowed on the bridge. Web site: www.grandcanyonskywalk.com.

DINING

Diamond Creek Restaurant, Route 66, Peach Springs. Part of the Huala-pai Lodge, this restaurant serves Native American favorites like fry bread, Native American stew, and Hualapai tacos. Pizza, hamburgers, and other sandwiches also appear on the menu. Beware of the pepper sauce on the table: it's spicy!

Delgadillo's Snow Cap, 301 E. Route 66, Seligman. Call 928-422-3291. You'll find "dead chicken" and "cheeseburgers with cheese" on the menu here and a sign that proudly declares, SORRY, WE'RE OPEN. The tongue-in-cheek humor doesn't end there. Want ice cream? Don't be surprised to get a bowl of ice with cream on top.

Mr. D'z Route 66 Diner, 105 E. Andy Devine Avenue/Route 66, Kingman.

Call 928-718-0066. Oprah fell in love with Mr. D'z homemade root beer when she made a surprise visit during a cross-country trip with best friend Gayle and turned this retro diner into a Route 66 icon. Try the baby back ribs doused in owner Armando Jimenez's homemade barbeque sauce. Web site: www.mrdzrt66 diner.com.

OTHER CONTACTS

Historic Route 66. This online resource provides detailed driving directions on where and how to retrace what remains of the precursor to I-40. Web site: www.historic66.com.

Hualapai Tourism, Peach Springs. Call 928-769-2636 or 1-888-868-9378. Plan your trip to Grand Canyon West, purchase tickets online, reserve a room at Hualapai Ranch, or schedule a rafting trip. Web site: www.grand canyonwest.com.

The Powerhouse Tourist Information & Visitor Center, 120 W. Route 66, Kingman. Call 928-753-6106 or 1-866-427-7866. Find information about Kingman and the surrounding area, including Seligman and Grand Canyon West, at the visitor center. The Powerhouse building also houses a museum dedicated to Route 66. Although the visitor center opens daily at 8, the museum doesn't open until 9. Both close at 5. Online, resources are available to help plan your visit. Web site: www.kingman tourism.org.

Seligman Chamber of Commerce, Seligman. Call 928-273-8140. Using the chamber's online resources, decide what to do and where to stay, eat, and shop while in Seligman. Web site: www.seligmanazchamber.com.

Horses along the side of the road near Chaco Canyon

OTHER RESOURCES

ARIZONA CONTACTS

AAA Arizona, 3144 N. 7th Avenue, Phoenix. Call 602-650-2700. Web site: www.aaaaz.com.

Arizona Association of Bed & Breakfast Inns. The association lists member bed & breakfasts as well as itineraries. Web site: www.arizona-bed-breakfast.com.

Arizona Association of RV Parks and Campgrounds, 428 E. Thunderbird Road, #548, Phoenix. Call 602-403-6196. An interactive map directs you to a listing of member RV parks, and campgrounds. Web site: www.az rvparks.com.

Arizona Game and Fish Department, 5000 W. Carefree Highway, Phoenix. Call 602-942-3000. Find information on fishing and hunting licenses, boating information, weekly fishing reports, and wildlife news. Web site: www.gf.state.az.us.

Arizona Highways Magazine, 2039 W. Lewis Avenue, Phoenix. Call 1-800-543-5432. Web site: www.arizona highways.com.

Arizona Hotel & Lodging Association, 1240 E. Missouri Avenue, Phoenix. Call 602-604-0729. The association lists member hotels, lodges,

and resorts and has a separate tab for certified green options. Web site: www.stayinaz.com.

Arizona Office of Tourism, 1110 W. Washington Street, #155, Phoenix. Call 1-866-275-5816. Web sites: www.azot.gov and www.arizona guide.com.

Arizona Restaurant Association. The association's online dining guide provides discounts, offers, and coupons. Web site: www.dine4az.com.

Arizona Road Conditions. Call 602-523-0244 or 1-888-411-7623. Web site: www.az511.gov.

Arizona State Parks, 1300 W. Washington Street, Phoenix. Call 602-542-4174. Web site: www.azstateparks .com.

COLORADO CONTACTS

Bed and Breakfast Innkeepers of Colorado. Call 1-800-265-7696. Locate an inn by amenities, city, nearby attractions, and special offers. Downloadable guides are available online. Web site: www.innsofcolorado.org.

Colorado Campground & Lodge Owners Association. Call 970-259-1899. Find a campground online or download a guide. Deals and promotions are also available online. Web site: www.campcolorado.com.

Colorado Department of Transportation. Call 303-639-1111. Web site: www.cotrip.org.

Colorado Division of Wildlife. Purchase your hunting or fishing license online, learn where to view wildlife, and find downloadable division of wildlife maps. Web site: www.wildlife.state.co.us.

Colorado Hotel & Lodging Association, 730 17th Street, #920, Denver. Call 303-297-8335. An interactive map makes it easy to pinpoint hotels and lodging by region. Web site: www.coloradolodging.com.

Colorado Tourism. Call 1-800-265-6723. Web site: www.colorado.com.

Colorado State Parks, 1313 Sherman Street, #618, Denver. Call 303-866-3437. Web site: www.parks.state.co.us.

NEW MEXICO CONTACTS

Indian Country New Mexico. Online resource with information on tribes, history, itineraries, and more. Web site: www.indiancountrynm.org.

New Mexico Association of RV Parks and Campgrounds. In addition to an online directory, the association's site provides a special-interest section that groups the RV parks and campgrounds by activities. Web site: www.newmexicorvparksand campgrounds.org.

New Mexico Bed and Breakfast Association. Call 1-800-661-6649. Browse by region, city, amenities, specials, and activities. Web site: www.nmbba.org.

New Mexico Department of Transportation. Call 1-800-432-4269. The site also provides links for road conditions in surrounding states, weather conditions, and flight delay information. Web site: www.nmshtd.state.nm.us.

New Mexico Game & Fish Department, One Wildlife Way, Santa Fe. Call 505-476-8000. You'll find information on hunting, fishing, bird watching, and off-highway vehicles. Web site: www.wildlife.state.nm.us.

New Mexico Lodging Association. Call 505-983-4554. The association has a simple site that includes specials. Web site: www.nmlodging.org.

New Mexico Magazine. Call 1-800-898-6639. Web site: www.nmmagazine.com.

New Mexico Restaurant Association, 9201 Montgomery NE, #602, Albuquerque. Call 505-432-0740 or 1-800-432-0740. The association's Web site features coupons, contests, and deals, covering all of New Mexico, El Paso, and Southern Colorado. Web site: www.southwestrestaurants.com.

New Mexico Tourism Department, 491 Old Santa Fe Trail, Santa Fe. Call

505-827-7400. Web site: www.new mexico.org

New Mexico State Parks Division, 1220 S. St. Francis Drive, Santa Fe. Call 505-476-3355 or 1-888-667-2757. Web site: www.emnrd.state.nm.us /prd.

UTAH CONTACTS

AAA Utah, 1400 S. Foothill Drive, #154, Salt Lake City. Call 801-238-1250. Web site: www.csaa.com.

Bed and Breakfast Inns of Utah. You can download a directory or search online. Web site: www.bbiu .org.

Utah Department of Transportation. Road condition information can be accessed by dialing 511 on any Utah-based phone. All other phones can access the information at 1-866-511-8824. Web site: www.udot.utah .gov.

Utah Division of Wildlife Resources, 1594 W. North Temple, #2110, Salt Lake City. Call 801-538-4700. The department offers online hunting and fishing licenses, information on animal species, fishing reports, hunting updates, podcast radio broadcasts, featured wildlife photos, and YouTube channel videos. Buy hunting and fishing licenses online and apply for hunt permits. Web site: www.wildlife.utah.gov.

Utah Hotel & Lodging Association. Call 801-593-2213. The site has links to lodging providers, campgrounds, guides, and outfitters. Web site: www .uhla.org.

Utah Office of Tourism, 300 N. State, Salt Lake City. Call 801-538-1030 or 1-800-200-1160. Web sites: www.travel .utah.gov or www.visitutah.com.

Utah State Parks, 1594 W. North Temple, #116, Salt Lake City. Call 801-538-7220. Web site: www.state parks.utah.gov.

OTHER CONTACTS

Indian Cultural Center, 2401 12th Street NW, Albuquerque, NM. Call 1-866-855-7902. The online site has information on New Mexico's 19 pueblos, including a list of feast days and dances. Web site: www.indian pueblo.org.

National Parks Service. In addition to learning about our national parks, you can purchase an $80 annual pass here that gives the pass owner and up to three accompanying adults free parking and entrance to the nation's parks and recreational lands. A $10 senior version is also available. Web site: www.nps.gov.

National Scenic Byways Program, 1200 New Jersey Avenue, SE, Washington, DC. The Web site lists nationally recognized scenic byways, state by state. Some byways have detailed information, maps, and itineraries. Others do not. Web site: www.byways .org.

A Native American boy performs a tribal dance. *New Mexico Tourism Department and Mike Stauffer*

SUGGESTED READING

Childs, Craig. *Finders Keepers: A Tale of Archaeological Plunder and Obsession.* New York, NY: Little, Brown and Company, 2010.

Childs, Craig. *House of Rain: Tracking a Vanished Civilization Across the American Southwest.* New York, NY: Back Bay Books, 2008.

Courlander, Harold. *The Fourth World of the Hopis: The Epic Story of the Hopi Indians as Preserved in Their Legends and Traditions.* Albuquerque, NM: University of New Mexico Press, 1987.

Daniels, Helen Sloan. *The Ute Indians of Southwestern Colorado.* Lake City, CO: Western Reflections Publishing Co., 2008.

De Mente, Boyé Lafayette and Demetra DeMent. *Visitors' Guide to Arizona Indian Reservations.* Phoenix, AZ: Phoenix Books/Publishers, 2010.

Dedera, Don. Navajo Rugs: *How to Find, Evaluate, Buy, and Care for Them.* Flagstaff, AZ: Northland Publishing, 1999.

Iverson, Peter. Dine: *A History of the Navajos.* Albuquerque, NM: University of New Mexico Press, 2002.

Kennard, Edward A. *Hopi Kachinas.* Walnut, CA: Kiva Publishing, 2002.

Kosik, Fran. Native Roads: *The Complete Motoring Guide to the Navajo and Hopi Nations.* Tucson, AZ: Rio Nuevo Publishers, 2003.

Linford, Laurance D. *Navajo Places: History, Legend, Landscape.* Salt Lake City, UT: The University of Utah Press, 2000.

Linford, Laurance D. *Tony Hillerman's Navajoland: Hideouts, Haunts and Havens in the Joe Leaphorn and Jim Chee Mysteries.* Salt Lake City, UT: The University of Utah Press, 2011.

Matthews, Washington. *The Mountain Chant: A Navajo Ceremony.* Salt Lake City, UT: The University of Utah Press, 2006.

McConnell, Virginia. *The Ute Indians of Utah, Colorado and New Mexico.* Boulder, CO: University Press of Colorado, 2000.

McManis, Kent. *Zuni Fetishes & Carvings.* Tucson, AZ: Rio Nuevo Publishers, 2010.

Noble, David Grant. *Ancient Ruins of the Southwest: An Archaeological Guide.* Flagstaff, AZ: Northland Publishing, 2000.

Plog, Stephen. *Ancient Peoples of the America Southwest.* New York, NY: Thames & Hudson, 2008.

The Animas River

Roberts, David. *In Search of the Old Ones: Exploring the Anasazi World of the Southwest.* New York, NY: Touchstone, 1997.

Simms, Steven R. *Traces of Fremont: Society and Rock Art in Ancient Utah.* Salt Lake City, UT: The University of Utah Press, 2010.

Trimble, Stephen. *The People: Indians of the American Southwest.* Santa Fe, NM: SAR Press, 1993.

Waters, Frank. *Book of the Hopi: The First Revelation of the Hopi's Historical and Religious Worldview of Life.* New York, NY: Penguin Books, 1977.

Wright, Margaret Nickelson. *Hopi Silver: The History and Hallmarks of Hopi Silversmithing.* Albuquerque, NM: University of New Mexico Press, 2003.

Cattle skulls for sale in Santa Fe

OTHER SITES IN THE SOUTHWEST

RUINS

Bandelier National Monument, 15 Entrance Road, Los Alamos, NM. Call 505-672-3861. More than 70 miles of trails take you to Ancestral Puebloan sites. Due to the 2011 Las Conchas Fire, which burned more than 50 percent of the park's landscape, much of the park is closed indefinitely. Hours are seasonal. The entrance fee is $12/vehicle. Web site: www.nps.gov /band.

Besh Ba Gowah Archeological Park, 1324 S. Jesse Hayes Road, Globe, AZ. Call 928-425-0320. Tour 700-year-old Salado ruins. Open daily 9–5. Admission is $5/adults, $4/ seniors, and free for children under 12. Web site: www.globeaz.gov /visitors/besh-ba-gowah.

Blackwater Draw National Historic Landmark, Clovis, NM. This extinct riverbed contains two ancient archaeological sites, including one of man's earliest attempts in the New World to control water.

Butler Wash Archeological Ruin, 14 miles south of Blanding, UT, on US 95. Call 435-587-1500. Hike to Ancestral Puebloan ruins that include dwelling structures and four kivas. www.blm.gov.

Casa Grande Ruins, Coolidge, AZ. Call 520-723-3172. Visit Hohokam ruins dating back to 1350 AD. Entrance fee of $5/person 16 and over. Web site: www.nps.gov/cagr.

Casa Malpais Archaeological Park, 318 E. Main Street, Springerville, AZ. Call 928-333-5375. The ruins situated on terraces of a fallen basalt cliff date to approximately 1300 A.D. Guided Tours daily at 9, 11, and 2.

Elden Pueblo, Flagstaff, AZ. Call 928-527-3452. Explore the ruins of a Sinagua village inhabited from 1070 to 1275 A.D.

Gila Cliff Dwellings, Silver City, NM. Call 575-536-9461. Guided tours to the 700-year-old ruins of the Mogollon people are offered daily at 1. Seasonal hours are posted online. Fee is $3/adult or $10/family. Web site: www .nps.gov/gicl.

Homolovi State Park, Winslow, AZ. Call 928-289-4106. This 150-room pueblo links the Ancestral Puebloans to today's Hopi villages. Web site: www.azstateparks.com/parks/horu.

Kinishba Ruins, Whiteriver, AZ. Call 520-338-4625. This pre-Columbian Mogollon ruin consists of nine masonry buildings that originally had 400–500 ground-floor rooms.

Montezuma Castle National Monument, Camp Verde, AZ. Call 928-567-3322. View a high-rise, 1,000-year-old ruin from the ground below. Open daily: 8–6 during the summer and 8–5 during the winter. The entrance fee is $5/adults. Web site: www.nps.gov/moca.

Mule Canyon Archaeological Ruin, Monticello, UT. Call 435-587-1500. You can walk around the 700-year-old Ancestral Puebloan ruins.

Palatki Heritage Site, Sedona. Call 928-282-3854. Near Sedona, you'll see cliff dwellings and rock art site. Red Rock Pass required ($5/day).

Pecos National Historic Park, Pecos, NM. Call 505-757-7200. You'll discover Pecos Pueblo and other pueblo ruins, a Spanish mission, and other historic sites. The park is open daily: 8–6 during the summer and 8–4:30 during the winter. Entrance fee is $3/person. Web site: www.nps.gov/peco.

Salinas Pueblo Missions National Monument, Mountainair, NM. Call 505-847-2585. At this site, you'll find partially excavated Tiwa ruins and four 17th century mission churches. Web site: www.nps.gov/sapu.

Tonto National Monument, AZ 188 near Lake Roosevelt, AZ. Call 928-467-2241. Hike to Salado cliff dwellings. The park is open daily 8–5. Admission is $3/person over 16. Web site: www.nps.gov/tont.

Tuzigoot National Monument, AZ. Call 928-634-5564. Visit the ruins of an ancient village built by the Sinagua culture. The monument is open daily: 8–6 during the summer and 8–5 during the winter. Admission is $5/adults. Web site: www.nps.gov/tuzi.

Walnut Canyon National Monument, AZ. Call 928-526-3367. Hike into Walnut Canyon to see 700-year-old cliff dwellings. The monument is open daily 9–5, but opens an hour earlier May through October. Admission is $5/person. Web site: www.nps.go/waca.

Wupatki National Monument, AZ. Call 928-679-2365. Eight hundred years ago, the Wupatki Pueblo was the largest around. The site is open daily 8–5. The cost is $5/person. Web site: www.nps.gov/wupa.

PETROGLYPHS

Buckhorn Wash Rock Art Panel, UT. Call 435-636-3600. Pictographs and petroglyphs stand out on these rock walls.

Petroglyph National Monument, Albuquerque, NM. Hike the trails to view a variety of petroglyphs. A small visitor center provides information on the trails and estimated 25,000 petroglyphs. There is no fee to visit the monument; however, it is co-managed with the City of Albuquerque, which charges $1/vehicle on weekdays and $2/weekends to park at Boca Negra Canyon. Web site: www.nps.gov/petr.

Newspaper Rock National Historic Site, UT. Call 435-587-1500. Two thousand years of human activity are recorded on the petroglyph panel here.

Sand Island Petroglyphs, 4 miles south of Bluff, UT. Call 435-587-1500. The sandstone cliff bears hundreds of 300- to 3,000-year-old petroglyphs.

Sego Canyon Rock Art and Ghost Town, UT. Call 435-259-2100. The canyon contains Fremont, Ute, and Barrier-style rock art. There's also a ghost town and the ruins of a coal mine.

Three Rivers Petroglyphs, NM. Call 575-525-4300. You'll find more than 21,000 petroglyphs at this New Mexico site.

V-Bar-V Heritage Site, Sedona, AZ. Call 928-282-3854. This is the largest known petroglyph site in the Verde Valley. Red Rock Pass is required ($5/day). The entrance gate is open 9:30–3. Web site: www.redrockcountry .org.

MUSEUMS, CULTURAL CENTERS, TRADING POSTS, AND MORE

The Amerind Museum, 2100 North Amerind Road, Dragoon, AZ. Call 520-586-3666. Located in Southern Arizona, off I-10, this museum houses an impressive collection of Indian artifacts, including the collection of founder William Shirley Fulton. Also on display are regional baskets, jewelry, pottery, kachinas, and a bow made and signed by Geronimo. The museum is open Tuesday through Sunday, 10–4. Admission is $8/adult, $7/seniors, $5/youth 12–8, and free for children under 12. Web site: www.amerind.org.

Center of Southwest Studies, 1000 Rim Drive, Durango, CO. Call 970-247-7456. Located on the Fort Lewis College, the exhibits here vary from local Native American history to fiber arts. Check online to see current exhibits. Web site: www.swcenter.ft lewis.edu.

Deer Valley Rock Art Center, 3711 W. Deer Valley Road, Phoenix, AZ. Call 623-582-8007. The mission of the Deer Valley Rock Art Center is to preserve and provide access to the Hedgepeth Hills petroglyph site, a collection of more than 1,500 petroglyphs, but there is also a museum here dedicated to the interpretation of petroglyphs and several rotating exhibits celebrating the Sonoran Desert. Outside, you'll also find the Neil Neilson Memorial Heritage Garden showcasing Native Americans crops like corn, tepary beans, chili peppers, and squash. The site has seasonal hours. Admission is $7/adults, $4/seniors and students, and $3/children 6–12. Web site: www .dvrac.asu.edu.

Edge of the Cedars State Park Museum, 600 W. North, Blanding, UT. Call 435-678-2238. Built on the site of an ancient village, the museum contains the largest collection of Ancestral Puebloan pottery in the Four Corners Area. Out back, you can view the village's restored kiva and dwelling structures. The park is open Monday through Saturday, 9–5. Admission is $5/adults, $3/children, or $20/family. Web site: www.stateparks .utah.gov/parks/edge-of-the-cedars.

Fremont Indian State Park Museum, 21 miles southwest of Richfield on I-70, UT. Call 435-527-4631. During the construction of I-70, workers uncovered the largest known Fremont Indian village. This museum preserves the pottery, baskets, arrowheads, and other artifacts discovered here. The park is open daily: 9–6 during the summer and 9–5 during the winter. Admission is $3/person or $6/vehicle. Web site: www.stateparks .utah.gov/parks/fremont.

Heard Museum, 2301 N. Central Avenue, Phoenix, AZ. Call 602-252-8848. The museum displays approximately 40,000 pieces of American Indian artwork in its 10 galleries, including 1,200 kachina dolls, and covers all Native American tribes throughout the country. It also hosts several events throughout the year, such as Spanish market, the World Championship Hoop Dance Contest, and the Guild Indian Fair & Market.

The museum is open Monday through Saturday, 9:30–5, and Sunday, 11–5. Admission is $15/adults, $13.50/seniors, and $7.50/students and children over 5. Web site: www .heard.org.

Huck's Museum and Trading Post, 1387 South Main, Blanding, UT. Call 435-678-2329. Privately owned and operated, the trading post also houses a museum displaying arrowheads, beads, pendants, and Ancestral Puebloan pottery. A fee is charged: $3/adult, $1.50/child. Open daily 8–5.

Indian Cultural Center, 2401 12th Street NW, Albuquerque, NM. Call 1-866-855-7902. The center's museum introduces you to the history of today's 19 Pueblos, beginning with their emergence stories. Displays of contemporary Puebloan art compliments the traditional artifacts exhibited. Although the center calls itself the gateway to the 19 pueblos of New Mexico, you can learn about tribes beyond the state's borders through special exhibits and daily dance performances. The center is open daily 9–5. You can visit for $6/adults and $3/children and students. Web site: www.indianpueblo.org.

Museum of Indian Arts & Culture, 710 Camino Lejo, Santa Fe, NM. Call 505-476-1250. Rotating exhibits explore regional Indians, past and present, through their art and artifacts. The museum is open Tuesday through Sunday, 10–5. From Memorial Day through Labor Day, it is also open on Monday, 10–5. Admission is $6/New Mexico residents and $9/nonresidents. Web site: www.miaclab.org.

Museum of Northern Arizona, 3101 N. Ft. Valley Road, Flagstaff, AZ. Call 928-774-5213. The museum focuses on the people, geology, and biology of the Colorado Plateau. Its award-winning permanent anthropology exhibit, *Native Peoples of the Colorado Plateau,* documents 12,000 years of human habitation. Other exhibits focus on the fine arts, including Native American arts. One of the museum's highlights is the replica kiva and modern Hopi mural. Open daily 9–5. Admission is $7/adults, $6/seniors, and $4/students. Web site: www.musnaz.org.

Pueblo Grande Museum and Archaeological Park, 4619 E. Washington Street, Phoenix, AZ. Call 602-495-0901. Inside, three galleries, including a hands-on children's gallery, showcase Hohokam artifacts. Outside, you can see Hohokam irrigation canals, an excavated ball court, platform mound and two full-scale reproductions of prehistoric Hohokam homes. The site is open Monday through Saturday, 9–4:45, and Sunday, 1–4:45. Admission is $6/adults, $5/seniors, and $3/children 6–17. Web site: www.phoenix.gov/PARKS/pueblo.html#INFO.

San Carlos Apache Culture Center, Milemarker 272 on US 70, AZ. Call 928-475-2894. The center tells the story of the Apache people and their history. It is open Monday through Friday, 9–5. Web site: www.sancarlosapache.com.

Smoki Museum, 147 N. Arizona Avenue, Prescott, AZ. Call 928-445-1230. Designed to resemble an Indian pueblo, the museum displays 4,000-year-old artifacts, Yavapai baskets, local pottery, models of dwellings, and kachina dolls. Open Monday through Saturday, 10–4, and Sunday, 1–4. Admission is $5/adults, $4/seniors, $3/students, and free for children under 12. Web site: www.smokimuseum.org.

Tohono O'odham Nation Cultural Center & Museum, Topawa, AZ. Call 520-383-0211. Displays the culture and history of the Tohono O'odham people.

Western New Mexico University Museum, Silver City, NM. Call 575-538-6386. The museum on the university campus contains a permanent display of Mimbres artifacts. It is open Monday through Friday, 9–4:30, and weekends 10–4. Web site: www.snmu.edu/univ/museum.shtml.

Wheelwright Museum of the American Indian, 704 Camino Lejo Santa Fe, NM. Call 505-982-4636 or 1-800-607-4636. The Wheelwright Museum collects objects and archives pertaining to the Navajo, Rio Grande

Pueblos and other native peoples of New Mexico, specializing in genres that other institutions generally overlook, like Navajo folk art. Hours are Monday through Saturday, 10–5, and Sunday, 1–5. Admission is free. Donations are appreciated. Web site: www .wheelwright.org.